Effective Discipline
in Secondary Schools
and Classrooms

Pamela Munn worked as a secondary school teacher in London before becoming a research fellow in the Education Department of Stirling University. She was involved in research on accountability in education and latterly on curriculum innovation before taking up a post as lecturer in applied research in education at York University where she was involved in helping teachers research their own schools and classrooms. Since 1986 she has been Depute Director of the Scottish Council for Research in Education. Her work there has included research on adult education, school boards and teacher recruitment.

Margaret Johnstone has been involved in educational research for sixteen years, working on a wide range of topics. Since 1986 she has been a researcher at the Scottish Council for Research in Education. Her work there has included a study of stress in teaching, a survey of truancy in secondary schools and the production of a package for teachers giving information on action against bullying.

Valerie Chalmers worked as a primary school teacher in a range of different schools before becoming involved in research into the training of primary school teachers. From that she moved on to join the research team investigating discipline in schools. She has now taken up a post in the Primary Development Department at Northern College of Education.

EFFECTIVE DISCIPLINE IN SECONDARY SCHOOLS AND CLASSROOMS

PAMELA MUNN

MARGARET JOHNSTONE

and

VALERIE CHALMERS

P·C·P

Paul Chapman
Publishing Ltd

Paul Chapman Publishing Ltd
144 Liverpool Road
London
N1 1LA

British Library Cataloguing in Publication Data
Munn, Pamela
  Effective discipline in secondary schools and classrooms.
  I. Title   II. Johnstone, Margaret, *1941*– III. Chalmers, Valerie
  373.11024

ISBN 1 85396 175 2

Typeset by Inforum Typesetting, Portsmouth
Printed and bound in Great Britain by
Athenaeum Press Ltd, Newcastle upon Tyne.
A B C D E F   7 6 5 4 3 2

CONTENTS

Contents

Advice

Prefects are nice,
And they give you advice.
Teachers will help you,
But the Janny will skelp you.

So when you get here,
Be full of good cheer,
And do what you're told,
And you'll live to be old.

(Jane, 1C)

PREFACE

This book has grown out of a research study commissioned by the Scottish Office Education Department (SOED). The three-year study investigated discipline in secondary and primary schools. Its focus was on understanding the policy and practice of a small number of schools. It set out to explore what these policies were and what had influenced them. It also studied experienced teachers in action in the classroom in an attempt to understand what they did to get their classes to work well.

The book and its companion volume *Effective Discipline in Primary Schools and Classrooms* offer teachers, teacher educators and advisers a framework for explaining why schools adopt particular approaches to discipline. They suggest a number of activities which schools could undertake to review their own practice and describe the benefits and costs of the policies in the research schools. At classroom level, they describe experienced teachers' practice, offer a framework for understanding that practice and suggest ways in which it could be used in pre-service and in-service training.

Discipline is a topic which has generated an extensive literature, ranging from small-scale sociological studies of individual schools and classrooms, and psychological studies using experimental and control groups, to the number-crunching approaches of large surveys of discipline. There have been more studies of indiscipline than of good discipline, as previous reviews of the literature have pointed out. Our research has concentrated on discipline and on what teachers and pupils see as contributing to good discipline.

There are some surprising omissions in the views we report. For example, there are few references to the curriculum as a factor promoting good discipline, perhaps because the common curriculum, mixed ability teaching and public examinations for all are now taken for granted. Similarly, there are few references to timetabling, physical features of the school, school size or links with social welfare agencies. Our open approach to collecting information and our emphasis on discipline rather than indiscipline may have led teachers to concentrate on matters of most immediate direct practical concern to them, such as the nature of their pupil population, rather than on espoused theories. We cannot, of course, claim that the frameworks we offer are comprehensive or complete, only that they are starting points for schools and teachers wanting to review their own practice. The book ends with a checklist of activities schools can undertake to explore their own practice. It argues that real and lasting improvements to discipline can only be made by understanding the influences on their current practice. We hope that teachers will be encouraged to look afresh at what they do and use the book as a springboard for ideas about developing and improving their school and classroom discipline.

ACKNOWLEDGEMENTS

This research was funded by the Scottish Office Education Department (SOED) whose support and encouragement is gratefully acknowledged. The research would not have been possible without the help and co-operation of the teachers and pupils in the case-study schools who spared time to be interviewed and who discussed our findings. Our particular thanks go to the teachers whose classroom practice we studied. Our project advisory commit-tee offered us constructive criticism and encouragement, and Janette Finlay typed successive drafts quickly and accurately. Dr Chris Holligan, a member of the research team for one year, helped to collect data in two of the schools.

The views and interpretations reported are those of the authors and are not necessarily those of SOED or the Scottish Council for Research in Education.

The authors and publishers would like to thank the following for giving their permission to reproduce material: Sally Brown and Donald McIntyre for permission to reproduce their work on teachers' goals and on procedures for analysing data on teachers' professional craft knowledge. Carfax Publishing Co. for permission to reproduce Munn, P., Johnstone, M. and Holligan, C. (1990) Pupils' views on effective disciplinarians, *British Educational Research Journal*, Vol. 16, no. 2, as part of Chapter 8.

1
EFFECTIVE DISCIPLINE

As every teacher knows, there is no infallible recipe for ensuring effective discipline. Instead, each school and teacher adopt a range of strategies which seem appropriate to their own particular circumstances and which are more or less effective. Teachers get few opportunities to hear about what happens outside their own classroom or school and when they do, the emphasis is on problem schools and pupils, not on success. Indiscipline, not good discipline, is what makes headlines and much of the writing on discipline concentrates on the causes of, and cures for, bad behaviour. It is relatively unusual for teachers to hear about what their colleagues are doing well and to learn about what encourages good practice.

This book describes practice in four secondary schools and explains how they promote and maintain effective discipline at two levels:

- whole school policy and practice;
- classroom policy and practice.

It sets out what is counted as effective discipline and the influences on these definitions. The schools had rather different approaches to discipline; in three of them the approach was seen as effective by staff and pupils. All of the schools had teachers who were seen by pupils as effective at getting their classes to work well. In describing what these schools and teachers did, it is not our intention that others should mimic their practice. Schools operate in particular contexts, with their own histories, and what works in one school or classroom will not necessarily work in another. Schools wanting to improve their discipline need to begin by understanding why their current practice is the way it is. Only then can they plan real and lasting improvements. This book provides a starting point for schools wanting to analyse their discipline policy and practice. It demonstrates that there were four key influences on discipline in the schools studied. These were:

- the schools' expectations about their pupils;
- what the teachers saw as the main purposes of teaching;
- the extent to which subject departments were free to set their own standards of discipline;
- the role of senior management.

Examples are provided of how these factors influenced discipline and we suggest things which teachers can do to detect the influence of these factors in their own schools. We also describe the rules, sanctions and rewards systems in operation in the four schools, the rather different role played by pastoral care in each and the part played by senior staff in promoting discipline. As in all human affairs, there are costs and benefits to any course of action; these are highlighted in relation to each school's approach as we go along and summarised at the end of each chapter.

At classroom level, the book describes what different teachers do to promote effective discipline and uses the similarities among the teachers' practice to construct a framework to understand their practice. This framework describes:

- the different kinds of actions teachers take, emphasising the importance of advance preparation and planning;
- the importance of the classroom context, particularly the teachers' beliefs about their pupils;
- the influence of teachers' goals for their classes and for individual pupils on teachers' actions.

Again, we are not suggesting that teachers mimic the actions described by the experienced teachers in the research project. Instead, we suggest that teachers wanting to think about and analyse their own classroom practice use the framework as a guide, which we see as being particularly useful to teacher educators and beginning teachers. We believe that only by teachers understanding what they do, and why they do it, will they have a sure basis for development and improvement.

The structure of the book

The book looks in turn at the issues described above. Chapters 2 to 5 discuss the key influences on the schools' definition of effective discipline and on the operation of discipline policy. They illustrate the rather different approaches used by the schools and sum up the benefits and costs of each. There is also a set of questions at the end of each chapter to stimulate discussion and some ideas for practical activities for teachers wishing to explore the assumptions underlying their school's approach to discipline.

Chapters 6 and 7 focus on classroom discipline. Chapter 6 contains the framework for understanding teachers' classroom practice and distinguishes two kinds of action to promote and maintain discipline: the proactive, taken to prevent disruption arising, and the reactive, designed to 'nip trouble in the bud' and avoid a problem escalating out of control. The framework then goes on to describe the influences on the actions teachers take, the most notable being what they know about their pupils and the goals they have for the class. Details of what teachers did and the most important kinds of goals and other influences on their actions are given in Chapter 7.

Chapter 8 concentrates on the pupils' views of school and classroom discipline. It describes the kinds of things which pupils believe their teachers do to get the class to work well and reveals that a wide range of actions are seen as effective. There is a surprising amount of unanimity among pupils in different schools about the kinds of rules which affect them most. Rules concerning dress and freedom of movement around the school seemed the most salient to pupils, regardless of which school they attended. However, some differences emerge when pupils discuss sanctions and rewards which in turn reflect the different expectations schools have of their pupils. This suggests to us that pupils are well aware of the assumptions that schools and teachers make about them.

Chapter 9 draws together the various influences on school discipline and shows how school and classroom discipline are connected. It contains a checklist of questions for senior staff to consider, drawn from the earlier chapters, and opens up the possibilities of a school investigating aspects of its own discipline policy and practice. There are now many texts offering advice to teachers wanting to research their schools and classrooms. Research can be an exhilarating, interesting and informative experience. To get most out of it, it needs to be carefully planned. If, as we hope, teachers are encouraged to research discipline policy and practice in their own schools, we urge them to take advice on planning and carrying out the research.

In an attempt to make the text 'user-friendly' we have avoided citing references to other authors, except where essential. A list of books and articles which we have found useful is given at the end of each chapter.

What is effective discipline?

We have already indicated that there is no universally agreed definition of effective discipline. It is, however, generally seen as having two distinct, if related, purposes. It is a means to an end, a necessary condition for learning. But it is also an end in itself. Discipline can be an *outcome* of schooling, socialising pupils into, for example, values of honesty, courtesy and regard for others. Interestingly enough, discipline as an end in itself was stressed far more by primary than secondary teachers. As Chapter 8 reveals, secondary school pupils tend to see discipline as a necessary state of affairs to get on with school work rather than as a virtue in its own right. There is agreement that what counts as effective discipline is heavily dependent on the context in which a teacher is operating. The age and stage of the pupils, the time of day, the time of year, the content of the lesson and many other factors can all have an influence. For example, effective discipline as seen by a teacher working with a group of sixth-year students about to sit their A-levels would be rather different from the discipline standard expected of first-year pupils. Similarly, what counts as effective discipline with first-years first thing on a Monday morning might not be the same last thing on a Friday afternoon. So, the same teacher can have different standards of discipline; teachers in the same school can have different standards; and teachers in different schools can have different standards.

Where does this leave us in our search for effective discipline? First of all, it highlights the futility of the quest for a universal answer or magic recipes to deal with discipline problems. What is appropriate in one school will not necessarily be appropriate in another. Schools have their own histories, their particular combinations of staff and pupils, their own cultures and circumstances which conspire to produce their particular approaches to discipline policy and practice. Second, however, an understanding of how schools operate their discipline policy and why they do so in particular ways, can sensitise us to aspects of school life that are perhaps taken for granted in the day-to-day hurly-burly. The emergence of similar influences on discipline policy among four rather different schools suggests that these are areas which schools could examine if they want to review their policy. Third, schools need a starting point to review their policy and practice. Since effective discipline is such a slippery concept and varies according to context, such a review needs an anchor which will direct an enquiry but at the same time not be unduly constraining by suggesting a particular view of what counts as effective discipline. Our research was guided by the following strategic questions. We list them here so that it is clear what kinds of concerns underpinned our enquiries of teachers and pupils. The questions may also be useful to a school interested in researching its own practice.

The first set of research questions concerned school rules and regulations. Work by many other writers in the area of discipline had suggested that underpinning the notion of discipline was a concern with rules and adherence to them. We therefore wanted to ask:

- What are the school rules?
- What are seen as the most important rules in practice?
- Who decides when the rules have been broken?
- Who decides what happens to rule breakers?

Since previous research on school discipline had indicated the importance of common standards in terms of rules, we were also interested in such questions as:

- Are common standards thought to be applied by staff?
- What factors are seen as affecting the implementation of common standards?

Finally, we were interested in the kinds of support that the school could offer when indiscipline had occurred and in any measures designed to promote good discipline. This was translated into such questions as:

- What is the role of the pastoral care system in promoting discipline and in reacting to indiscipline?

- What kinds of punishments are used?
- How effective are the support systems perceived to be?

These were the questions which guided our enquiry into school discipline. For classroom discipline we used a more open approach. We did not want teachers to suppose that we had a predetermined idea of what effective discipline would look like in their classrooms. Nor did we wish them to think and talk about only punitive or authoritarian strategies. In our view, effective classroom discipline was something which allowed learning to take place. This was translated into a single interview question with teachers, 'What did you do to get the class to work well?'. We were clear that effective discipline was not the same as effective learning. A teacher could have effective discipline without necessarily promoting and encouraging pupils to learn whatever was intended. Clearly, a teacher's knowledge about the topic of the lesson, the clarity and quality of exposition and the matching of these to what pupils already know and can do are all influences on effective learning. Can pupils learn if there is no discipline in the classroom? The answer to this must be that, at a minimum, effective learning is severely impeded if the teacher has little or no control over the pupils' behaviour. Effective discipline appeared to be a necessary, if not sufficient, pre-condition of effective learning.

It is important to distinguish effective discipline from effective learning if teachers are interested in researching their own classroom practice, so that the focus of their research is clear. Our approach was to concentrate on the actions teachers took and the influences on these actions. Teachers wanting to research their practice could note their actions with a particular class, preferably one with which they feel happy and confident, over a couple of lessons. They could note the influence on these actions and the goals they had for the class and/or for individual pupils. Alternatively, a pair of teachers could work together, helping each other to describe their actions and the influences on them.

We had no objective measures of whether the class did work well, beyond our own observations. Our starting point was the individual teacher's definition. We can say from our observations that the pupils seemed busy and productive. The classrooms were enjoyable and interesting places to be and we witnessed no major incidents of indiscipline such as verbal or physical abuse among teachers or pupils.

Do schools make a difference?

This book makes the assumption that there are ways in which schools and teachers can affect the behaviour of their pupils. Is this a well-founded assumption? The short answer is 'yes', although it is only in the relatively recent past that schools have come to be seen as social institutions, whose nature and climate have important influences on the behaviour, attitudes and attainments of pupils and, indeed, of teachers. Much of the recent research on school effectiveness has shown that schools do make a difference and that schools with similar pupil intakes and catchment areas can produce rather different results, not only in the academic achievements of their pupils but in the behaviour of their pupils as well.

Clearly, pupils' home backgrounds and their local communities are very important influences on their behaviour and values. We are by no means suggesting that these are neutral elements in a school's quest for effective discipline, or indeed, in other aspects of school life. However, it is more difficult for schools to influence their pupils' backgrounds and community culture than their own practice.

Schools can do much within their own boundaries to promote effective discipline. This is not to say that involving parents and the local community is unimportant. Far from it. We suggest that schools could, with profit, examine the tenor and frequency of their communications with parents. It was striking, however, that the secondary teachers we interviewed made very few references to the role of parents in promoting good discipline in their schools. Our own attempts to gather parents' views about effective discipline were fraught with difficulty and we did not have the resources necessary to allow home visits which would have produced more systematic and reliable information. There is overwhelming research evidence about the beneficial effects on pupils' learning of parental involvement. It seems to us that an important aspect of such involvement is in the values which parents portray about schooling. Schools, of course, have values too and these are reflected in its discipline policy. An important point for any school wanting to improve its discipline is to involve parents in the process. The vast majority of parents want their children to do well at school and have a happy and enjoyable experience. A benefit of greater parental participation could be sharing of home and school values, which in turn could have positive effects on discipline.

Before describing the schools' different approaches to discipline and the influences on their approaches, we need to say a little about the schools themselves and the way we collected information about their policy and practice.

The schools

The four schools involved in the research were comprehensives in two different Regional Education Authorities in Scotland. We chose regions and schools which were, in some sense, typical of Scotland. One of the authorities included a sub-division covering a large city, which in common with most British cities had areas of multiple deprivation. The other authority contained a mixture of small and large towns as well as rural areas. Within these two authorities we wanted to choose schools which were, again, typical but which would provide us with a contrast. How one chooses a typical school is a vexed question, as all schools have claims to individuality and uniqueness. We based our choice on size, by calculating the average size of schools in the two authorities and selecting those which matched this. However, our choice was not quite a random one. In the inner city the contrast we sought was between a Roman Catholic school and a non-denominational school. Both of these urban schools had catchment areas characterised as areas of multiple deprivation. In the other authority the contrast was between a school in a large town and another in a small town where it was the only secondary school in the area. Each of the schools is described in a little more detail below. They have been given fictitious names.

St James is a Roman Catholic co-educational school located in the east end of one of Scotland's largest cities. Official statistics reveal that the school's widely dispersed catchment area contains some 78 per cent of pupils from 'areas of priority treatment'. In recognition of this the school has above average staffing ratios to help pupils with learning difficulties. In common with many secondary schools, the pupil roll has fallen dramatically during the past few years and stands at nearly 700. The school has the physical capacity for over 1,000 pupils. There is a prefect system. The headteacher had been in post for over five years when we conducted the research. Most teaching staff have worked in the school for a number of years and staff turnover is low. The school has a total of 55 teachers. There is a roughly even balance between male and female staff, although the school's senior management are all male.

Easthill is a non-denominational comprehensive situated on the edge of parkland on the outskirts of the same large city as St James. Its situation is somewhat unusual since it lies a mile and a half outside its catchment area. This catchment area also contains a large percentage of pupils from areas of multiple deprivation and, again, this is recognised in the provision of additional staff. The school has a much smaller roll than St James, about 400 pupils, although it has the physical capacity for over 1,000. Our size criterion of typicality went somewhat awry here, due to a variety of circumstances. Having established contact with the school and obtained the permission of the authority to undertake the research, we were reluctant to abandon it. There are 43 teachers with a fairly even split between the sexes. Once again, however, the senior management staff are all male and comprise an acting headteacher (who has been depute (deputy) head) and two assistant headteachers. Easthill also has a Pupil Support Unit (PSU) whose function is, according to the school handbook, 'to provide a strong support for both staff and pupils . . . in order to enhance learning and discipline in the school.' The unit is staffed by two teachers and has the additional services of two educational psychologists and a social worker.

Braidburn is the only secondary school serving a small industrial town, geographically rather cut off from the rest of the region. The town is tied to a declining industry but there have been a small number of 'incomers' whose children attend the school. The headteacher described his pupils as 'solidly working class.' Most of the pupils come from long established families in the town and there is a small intake of pupils from the rural hinterland. The school occupies two buildings, one considerably more modern than the other. It is school policy that all pupils have lessons in each building. There are around 900 pupils on roll. The school has a prefect system, the fifth- and sixth-year pupils being eligible for election by their peers. It also has a 'progress unit' as it is called in the school, a special unit for children with severe learning and/or social problems. There are 64 teachers in the school, roughly evenly divided between men and women. Staff turnover is low with a few teachers having been in the school for over fifteen years. At the time of the research, the well established headteacher had just retired and a new head had been appointed. The school's five senior management staff are, again, all male.

Oldtown is an old academic foundation, formerly a selective school which became comprehensive in 1970. It stands on the outskirts of a large Scottish town. Its catchment area is largely composed of owner-occupied houses with some local authority housing and rural areas of farms and villages. Pupils on roll number just over 900, which means that the school has been able to dispense with the huts it had to use when its roll went up to 1,200 in the mid 1980s. There is a prefect system, the prefects being chosen by the teachers. There are 62 teachers, evenly split between men and women. Staff turnover is almost non-existent, being confined to the retirement of senior staff. The headteacher has been in post for about five years. Oldtown's senior management team is distinctive in that it contains one woman, although as an 'acting' assistant headteacher, among its staff of five.

How did we collect information about the schools' discipline policy and practice?

To investigate school policy and practice we used the following approaches:

- interviews with a variety of teachers (see Table 1.1);
- pupils' writing about school rules, sanctions and rewards;
- analysis of school documents, such as the brochure, staff handbook and other material on discipline;
- notes on school life, often called 'field notes' in case study research.

Details about all these approaches, and about the ways in which we analysed the information collected, are given in the research appendix (page 129). For the moment, all we need stress is that teachers in five main subject departments were interviewed. These departments were English, mathematics, science, physical education and either art or music. They were chosen as likely to be illustrative of a range of concerns about discipline. Some departments, for example, would be highly conscious of safety requirements as their subjects involved handling potentially dangerous materials, or a good deal of movement among pupils. Others involved pupils in more sedentary work where discipline concerns were likely to be different. In each department, the head of department was interviewed and two other staff, chosen at random. We also interviewed senior management staff and those teachers with specific responsibilities for pastoral care. The interviews were carried out in private, almost all were tape recorded and they lasted on average about an hour.

Table 1.1: Numbers of staff interviewed

Headteacher	Senior Management	Heads of Department	Teachers	Other	Total
4	13	32	35	3	87

We used the following approaches to study classroom discipline:

- pupils' writing about what their teachers did to get the class to work well;
- observation of sixteen teachers over about a fortnight, teaching two different classes;
- interviews with each of these teachers after each observed lesson to elicit from them what they had done to get the class to work well.

What can we learn from the intensive study of four schools?

Our study of four schools revealed rather different approaches to discipline among them, which were seen as effective by the staff because of the types of schools they were. In the chapters which follow, these approaches are described and their benefits and costs are analysed. As important as *what* these schools did, however, is *why* they used their particular approaches. One of the benefits of an intensive study of a small number of schools is that it should be possible to discover the rationale for using particular policies. One of the most interesting things to emerge from our study was that although the schools had *different* approaches, these were underpinned by the *same* kinds of influences. For example, expectations about pupils influenced the different approaches all the schools took. This suggests that schools wanting to review their discipline need to analyse many things which they necessarily have to take for granted in the day-to-day business of school life. They need to analyse what expectations they have about their pupils by looking afresh at their school brochure, at the rules which are seen to be important and the sanctions that are most frequently used, and at the hidden messages conveyed by all these elements. They also need to consider whether they have any rewards for good behaviour. It was striking that punishments for bad behaviour were much more in evidence than rewards for good behaviour.

The study of these schools, then, helps us to:

- describe the different approaches to discipline used;
- identify the aspects of school life which need to be reviewed and examined before discipline policy and practice can be changed effectively.

We hope that the experiences of the schools strike chords about practice in readers' own schools and will stimulate discussion and debate about why things are the way they are. It is very difficult to look at a familiar institution through the eyes of a stranger and to question aspects of school life that have to be taken for granted. It is also fascinating and enlightening.

It is similarly revealing and rewarding to analyse one's own teaching or the teaching of colleagues from the starting point of what is being done to get the class to work well. There are so many reports of what teachers are not doing that they ought to be doing, that it is all too easy to neglect the routine, spontaneous actions which experienced teachers use to promote learning. As experienced teachers begin to play an ever more prominent role in the education of novices, it is surely vital that they come to understand their own classroom practice more fully and, indeed, how they came to acquire their expertise. Clearly, experienced teachers need to know about their own practice before they can pass on the elements of their craft to newcomers. This is harder than it seems, for the busyness and demanding nature of teaching do not encourage quiet reflection or discussion about practice.

Finally, it can also be revealing to collect information from pupils about their view of school discipline. Many of the teachers in the case-study schools were sceptical about our attempts to collect information in this way. They were pleasantly surprised at the seriousness and thoroughness with which pupils answered our questions. Indeed, one of the best research experiences we have had was feeding back to teachers what their pupils had to say about their classroom practice. Obviously it is more difficult for teachers than outsiders to collect information from pupils, particularly about classroom practice. Such an exercise would need to be carefully set up and explained. Perhaps it is more feasible for schools to collect information from pupils about their views of school rules, sanctions and rewards and the strengths and weaknesses of the school's discipline. They are an important and often neglected source of information about many aspects of school life. A small-scale pilot exercise with a couple of classes is a way of assessing the value of such an exercise.

Table 1.2: Characteristics of the four case-study schools

	St James (Roman Catholic comprehensive)	Easthill (non-denominational comprehensive)	Braidburn (non-denominational comprehensive)	Oldtown (non-denominational comprehensive)
CATCHMENT AREA	• dispersed, not close to the school • area of multiple deprivation	• not close to the school • area of multiple deprivation	• an integral community • area of declining industry	• suburban community, close to the school • area of high levels of home ownership, some council housing
SCHOOL ROLL	• under capacity • actual roll, 700	• under capacity • actual roll, 400	• at capacity • actual roll, 900	• at capacity • actual roll, 950
STAFFING	• above average to take account of pupil intake	• above average to take account of pupil intake • pupil support unit within the school	• average • special unit for pupils with severe learning and/or social problems	• average
HEADTEACHER	• in post for 5 years • previous experience in similar schools	• none in post, acting headteacher experience in Easthill	• headteacher retiring after 17 years in post • previous experience in similar school	• in post for 5 years • previous experience in similar school
BUILDINGS	• modern, one building • no playing field beside the school	• modern, one building • green field site	• Victorian building and modern building: split site • green field site	• modern, one building • green field site
HISTORY	• formerly run by Marist brothers • perceived as 'difficult' in the past	• steeply declining roll • staff worried about closure • seen as having gone through a difficult past	• former 'academy' • in the past had a poor reputation • currently perceived as a 'good' school locally	• former 'academy,' • long academic tradition • perceived as a 'good' school locally and nationally

References

Some useful books about discipline and school effectiveness:

Denscombe, M. (1985) *Classroom Control: A Sociological Perspective*, Allen & Unwin, London.

Department of Education and Science (1989) *Discipline in School, (The Elton Report)*, DES/HMSO, London.

Docking, J. W. (1989) *Control and Discipline in Schools: Perspectives and Approaches*, Paul Chapman, London.

Galloway, D., Ball, T., Bloomfield, D. and Seyd, R. (1982) *Schools and Disruptive Pupils*, Longman, London.

Gray, J., McPherson, A. F. and Raffe, D. (1983) *Reconstructions of Secondary Education: Theory, Myth and Practice since the War*, Routledge & Kegan Paul, London.

Johnstone, M. and Munn, P. (1987) *Discipline in school: A review of 'causes' and 'cures'*, Scottish Council for Research in Education, Edinburgh.

McPherson, A. F. and Willms, J. D. (1987) Equalisation and improvement: some effects of comprehensive reorganisation in Scotland, *Sociology*, 21, 4, pp 509–40.

Mortimore, P. (1983) *Achievement in Schools*, ILEA: Research and Statistics Branch, London.

Peters, R. S. (1966) *Ethics and Education*, Allen & Unwin, London.

Reynolds, D. (1985) *Studying School Effectiveness*, Falmer Press, Lewes.

Rutter, M., Maughan, B. Mortimore, P. and Ouston, J. (1979) *Fifteen Thousand Hours: Secondary Schools and their Effects on Children*, Open Books, London.

Some useful books about teacher research:

Holly, P. and Southworth, G. (1989) *The Developing School*, Falmer Press, Lewes.

Hopkins, D. (1990) *Evaluation for School Development*, Open University Press, Milton Keynes.

Lewis, I. and Munn, P. (1987) *So You Want to do Research! A Guide for Teachers on how to Formulate Research Questions*, Scottish Council for Research in Education, Edinburgh.

Munn, P. and Drever, E. (1990) *Using Questionnaires in Small-Scale Research: A Teachers' Guide*, Scottish Council for Research in Education, Edinburgh.

Walker, R. (1985) *Doing Research: A Handbook for Teachers*, Methuen, London.

2

THE SCHOOL'S VIEW
OF ITS PUPILS

In Chapter 1 we suggested that particular ideas held by teachers within any school can influence the school's policies. The ideas emerged from the data taken from four case-study schools. These schools were working within their own contexts and for good reasons adopted a particular policy and practice which seemed to staff to be necessary. The key idea discussed in this chapter is that: *schools view their pupils in particular and distinctive ways and these views affect discipline policy and practice.*

This chapter suggests that in order to analyse and improve upon any school's discipline policy, staff must examine carefully their own working arrangements. They must do this in order to identify the hidden agendas which underlie day-to-day rules, sanctions, rewards and all the other means used to promote and maintain effective discipline.

This idea that we, as teachers, define pupils in a particular way may seem rather contentious. It may, for one thing, smack of 'labelling'. We may be happier with the thought that most schools use similar arrangements for promoting good discipline. After all, secondary schools in Britain surely have the same broad aims for their pupils. These can be summed up as furthering academic achievement, preparing pupils for adult life, helping them to develop their social skills and an emotional maturity, and rational autonomy. If, then, these are aims which all schools hold in common, how can it be that schools view pupils in particular and distinctive ways? The answer lies in the subtle degrees of emphasis given to some aims rather than others. So, we argue that though all schools will have these overall aims in common, how they apply their discipline policies sets up a distinctive view of their pupils. As we will demonstrate from our own case-studies, the emphasis on particular rules and behaviour differed quite sharply among the four schools.

Before describing these differences, let us first be clear about what we mean by the school's definition of its pupils. This notion of a school view sets up a notion of consensus, even the idea that it is static and unchanging. Of course, we know that neither of these suppositions is true. Where do we find consensus? How can you, as a teacher, examine your own school view? We found that a telling way of doing this was to look closely at the various documents which every school has. These would include:

- the school prospectus/brochure;
- documents listing school rules;
- policy documents on discipline intended for staff.

We studied the above to see where the similarities and the differences were. We also examined the use of sanctions and rewards, and how and for which pupils the pastoral care system operated. Another element in establishing a school's view of its pupils is what the teachers have to say about them. In all four schools, teachers had a great deal to say about their pupils' abilities, interests, friendship groups and home backgrounds. Indeed, as we shall see in Chapters 6 and 7, this knowledge directly affected their classroom discipline. All teachers have a great deal of knowledge and understanding about their pupils and many will talk at length and with enthusiasm about them. Their descriptions and explanations are often good indications of the way the school defines its pupils and how the individual pupil measures up to this. Apart from teacher talk, our evidence for establishing a school view was taken from daily observations of the ways in which the discipline structure operated within the school, for example: which school rules were considered to be important; what kinds of punishments were used when particular rules were broken; and which type of roles were thought to be appropriate for pastoral care staff.

All of the above sources of evidence are available to staff who wish to examine their own school's practice to discover what is their particular view of the pupil.

It seemed to us that, taken together, all these sources of evidence presented us with a clearly defined and distinctive view of the different emphases within the discipline systems, reflecting the four schools' different views of their pupils. Of course, we do not suggest that these schools – or any other – proclaim a particular view, but we do claim that each of our schools had an intrinsic view; it had permeated the woodwork of the school, was taken for granted by staff and pupils alike and was largely unquestioned. Un-surprisingly, perhaps, those most conscious of the fact that there was a par-ticular view were those teachers who did not wholly subscribe to it. They were least comfortable with this view and did not feel able to take it for granted. How did our schools see their pupils?

St James was a Roman Catholic comprehensive school located in a large urban area with a high percentage of pupils from disadvantaged areas. Staff turnover was low and though the school roll had fallen in recent years, it had become relatively stable. The headteacher had been in post for five years. St James had a view of its pupils as members of the school family. This family had a hierarchy, some members carried greater influence than others but essentially pupils were seen as belonging to a friendly, welcoming group.

Braidburn, the only comprehensive serving a small, somewhat isolated industrial town, had an intake of pupils described as coming from 'solid working-class' backgrounds. Staff turnover was low with a well-established headteacher who was retiring at the time of the research. Braidburn had a view of its pupils as younger members of the community.

Easthill was a non-denominational comprehensive situated outside its catchment area, taking a large percentage of pupils from areas of multiple deprivation. Its roll had fallen dramatically and the school, as a result, had had to shed many of its staff. Easthill had a view of its pupils as socially deficient.

Oldtown, an old academic foundation, became comprehensive in 1970. Its catchment area was largely composed of middle class homes, though a minority of pupils came from local authority housing and the rural areas. The school roll was fairly static while staff turnover was virtually non-existent and confined largely to retirement of long-serving staff. Oldtown had a view of its pupils as scholars.

As already mentioned, not everyone agreed with the way pupils were viewed. It can be instructive to talk to members of staff who do not subscribe to the dominant view. They can often provide a more comprehensive picture than those who are firmly wedded to the main body of opinion.

Let us now look at how these views were put into operation through the various discipline and organization structures of the school. We hope that these sources of evidence will be helpful to schools researching their own practice.

The school brochure

Throughout the country schools spend time and effort producing brochures which portray a certain image of their school. As we indicated earlier, all schools have broadly similar aims for their pupils and these are set out in their brochures. There were some basic similarities among the brochures in the four schools but there were also some quite marked differences in emphases, which seemed to us to be related to the primary purposes of schooling.

The brochure at Oldtown stated that the school's aim was 'to equip [pupils] to be successful in examinations and to let [pupils] leave school with the confidence and ability to cope with life in the world outside'. The identification of academic achievement as an important aim of the school was a central theme of the brochure. Considerable space, for example, was given to such matters as the formal curriculum, methods of assessment, the importance of homework to 'foster the study habit' and communication between parents and school on pupils' progress and attainment. Pupil motivation, attitudes, behaviour and welfare were also mentioned but the over-riding theme was academic achievement. The emphasis placed on this was evident not only in the headteacher's first sentence of an open letter to pupils – 'Welcome to one of Scotland's oldest and most famous schools' – but also in the mention of specific prizes and awards: 'The school awards prizes and trophies to pupils for distinguished performance in academic, athletic and sporting activities ... the pupil judged to be the most academically distinguished in S5 [fifth year] is awarded the . . . gold medal instituted in 1879.

Interestingly, too, and very much in line with this definition of the pupil, the staff list contained within the brochure detailed all the degrees and diplomas held by each of the teachers. This may seem a small point, but none of the other brochures in the case-study schools did so. The brochure of Oldtown characterised the school's view of its pupils as scholars. As far as discipline was concerned, the brochure assumed that pupils would know the meaning of good behaviour. Specific rules did not need to be spelt out:

> Pupils are expected to behave in a reasonable and orderly manner at all times in and around the school and on the way to and from school. They are expected to deal fairly with one another and to show consideration for others – pupils, staff and members of the public. They are expected to be neat and tidy in appearance.

In contrast, in St James and Braidburn, the social and emotional growth of pupils was stressed as much as their scholastic achievement. Similarly, at both schools pupils were viewed as biddable, though not necessarily well-motivated towards academic work. Neither intake was seen as particularly interested in the traditional curriculum and the school brochures reflected a view of their pupils which suggested that other aspects of development were as important as academic merit. The brochures let it be known that the school's interest in pupils extended beyond the confines of the school and that the development of the 'whole child' was important:

> The young people of the area are the responsibility of school, parents and community. School interest does not cease at 4.00 pm; the community interest should not cease at 9.00 am. . . . It is only by working together, by appreciating each other's work and problems that we can meet the aims of the school and make ours a happy, efficient community.

In St James, which drew its pupils from a widely dispersed area because it was the only Roman Catholic school in that particular locality, the school's emphasis on a view of pupils as family was based on a shared religious faith rather than on geography. The brochure's description of the school reflects this family feeling: 'The school is a close-knit community of pupils, parents and teachers and seeks the support of the family in educating all the young persons in its area. [We are] a Catholic school community and the study and observance of the faith is practised daily'.

In our fourth school, Easthill, the view was different again. Though the school drew its pupils from a similar area as St James – an area with high levels of multiple deprivation – there was, as far as Easthill was concerned, no unifying factor. The catchment area and falling school roll, together with the turbulent history of the school, encouraged a view of its pupils as deficient in the kinds of social skills which Oldtown could take for granted. This was reflected in the way in which the school presented itself. The brochure set out clearly the rules of good behaviour precisely because these could not, as far as the school was concerned, be taken for granted. It also set out the consequences of rule-breaking behaviour. Note the different emphasis in the tone of the Easthill brochure:

> Within the classroom pupils are expected to bring the equipment needed for their lessons, to return homework on time and behave in such a way that their work can be done without disturbing others. Any pupil failing to do this will normally be given a row (reprimand) and warned that unless they improve they will be punished.

In Easthill, pupils were seen as not sharing the same social and behavioural values as teachers in the school. There were 'their values' and 'our values'. The emphasis, therefore, in the brochure, was on detailing the consequences of breaking the rules. A section in Easthill's brochure dealing with the 'conduct system' set out the successively more serious punishments to be used in the event of bad behaviour:

> A row is followed by punishment exercises which become longer and more numerous in the event of non-completion. . . If a pupil fails to return all three exercises he will be sent home by the Depute Headteacher and will not be accepted back into school until the parents have seen [the Depute] and all three exercises have been done.

There then follow details of suspension and official exclusion from school. The tone throughout is of firmness, but there is also the expressed expectation of 'trouble' from pupils. The message which the school brochure conveys is of pupils who do not naturally adhere to acceptable rules of social behaviour. The school's definition of its pupils which came across clearly from the brochure was of pupils as socially deficient.

Of course, we are not claiming that this dominant view of pupils as portrayed in the brochure was the only one held. We recognised that, in these schools, teachers had many aims for their pupils. However, we believe that some aims were given prominence over others and that, because of this, there were important effects on how the discipline policy operated. What do we mean by this? How can a particular view taken of the pupils affect how schools operate their discipline system? We suggest that the rules which are prominent and the way they are explained and enforced are directly affected by the way pupils in the school are viewed. Staff in any secondary school are able to look at their own practice and consider what hidden messages are being delivered. This is no easy task, of course. Consideration of the points at the end of this chapter may help. Let us now look at the different rule systems in our case-study schools.

Rules

All schools have rules to guide the conduct of their pupils and many of these are specified not by the school but by the Education Authority as the body legally responsible for providing education. There were, therefore, many rules which our four schools had in common. These included safety procedures, attendance and the procedures for notifying absence from school, and the care of property and equipment. It may be argued that as far as social behaviour is concerned all secondary schools have very similar rules to do with respecting the rights of other people and treating them as you would expect to be treated. We would agree with all of this and, indeed, we found many social rules were held in common. Where the case-study schools differed was in the importance given to some rules and in the way these were transmitted and applied.

The rules at Easthill tended to be written in terms of warnings of the consequences of bad behaviour rather than in conveying a sense of high expectation, as we found in our other schools. Pupils were seen as having little prospect of behaving well as a matter of course. The rule system, therefore, had to be clear as to the consequences of bad behaviour. The contrast between rules at Easthill and at Oldtown was stark. In Oldtown, the staff stressed rules associated with willingness to work, such as homework being done on time and quiet movement round the corridors to facilitate good working conditions. In contrast, the Easthill teachers' emphasis was on the need to protect school property by enforcing rules about out-of-bounds areas.

More subtle, perhaps, was the way in which rules were communicated to pupils. This, in itself, revealed much about how the school viewed its pupils. In St James, for example, where the pupils were regarded as members of the school family, the rules and, crucially, the rationale for these rules, were conveyed through the social education programme. Some of the lessons within this programme were devoted to discussion between teachers and pupils of 'good' and 'bad' rules. This was based on a view of pupils which, while understanding the disadvantages of their backgrounds, saw them as innately capable of good behaviour: a belief which accorded with the principle of a shared Catholic faith. A typical comment from a St James teacher on the pupils' reactions to rules was that: 'Once they [pupils] understand that there's a practical reason for the rule, they accept it'.

This is in sharp contrast to the views taken by staff at Oldtown and Easthill. In both schools, rules were generally enforced without great attention being paid to explanation of the rationale. However, the reasons for this were totally opposed. At Oldtown, pupils were not expected to require an explanation both because the home provided this and because the school's role was to provide an academic menu. Rules at Oldtown were copied out into jotters in much the same way as homework would be copied down. At Easthill, pupils were viewed as being so far 'beyond the pale' that only the consequences of rule breaking would deter them. The differences between these views were illustrated by a teacher at Easthill: '[Pupils] just come right up against the rules and that's how they find out that that's a rule – when they've broken it'.

The implication of the above comment was that pupils were so far removed from what was seen by school staff as acceptable behaviour that it would be impossible for the school to specify all the ways in which a pupil should behave. The school's justification for taking this view was given by a teacher:

'The school serves an area of massive deprivation by any criteria – [numbers of] single parent families, [levels of] high unemployment, alcoholism, drug abuse. This does influence the way pupils are dealt with'.

There is a contrast here with Oldtown where pupils were encouraged to accept the rules, not only because they were familiar, but because they were being transmitted by people in authority in much the same way as subject knowledge was transmitted. A teacher at Oldtown explained: 'Yes, they [pupils] do respect the rules. They're never encouraged not to. There's not an atmosphere of questioning the rules'.

So far, we have suggested that the kind of rules which predominated in our case-study schools reflected the schools' views of their pupils. While each view was different, this led teachers in each of the schools to apply the rules in a particular way. They also communicated the rules in distinctive ways which were dependent on how they viewed these pupils. We have pointed out, for example, that Oldtown emphasised work rules and conveyed these rules in the same way as subject knowledge was conveyed. Just as pupils were expected to accept subject knowledge, they were expected to accept these rules. In Braidburn and St James the salience of rules centring on courtesy and respect for others was paramount.

Further, these schools' views of their pupils encouraged debate and discussion on the rationale for the rules in the belief that once this was evident, the children would more readily subscribe to such rules. In Easthill, the socially deficient view which predominated led to rules being couched in terms of 'warnings' and 'consequences' as a deterrent.

Our aim in outlining the differences between the rules in schools has not been to criticise or to praise. The purpose has been to show the influence on rules of expectations about pupils. The way the rules are explained and applied has both benefits and costs for each school. In Oldtown, for example, where rules were conveyed formally, the benefit to staff and pupils was that the message was clear and unequivocal and time was not 'wasted' on discussion and debate. One of the costs of this, however, was that some pupils might fail to understand such an unequivocal system. The possible outcome could be that some pupils become alienated from the rules and, ultimately, the school. The view of pupil as scholar, prevalent at Oldtown, might not fit with the reality of all pupils.

At Braidburn and St James, where rules were conveyed both formally and also discussed and explained, the pupils were more likely to understand the rationale for the rules and the need to apply these strictly. One of the costs, however, for these schools might be the time involved for discussion, at the expense of other areas of the curriculum. In Easthill, a benefit was that pupils were left in no doubt as to the consequences of rule breaking. A major cost, however, of interpreting the system in this way was that to pupils rules equated with punishment. The result could also be that the system for dealing with rule-breakers became overloaded and unworkable. Rules at Easthill, because of the negative way they were conveyed, had become inextricably linked with sanctions. Of course, the other case-study schools also had a system of sanctions. Let us now consider how these operated.

Sanctions

Just as all schools have rules to guide the conduct of pupils, they also have sanctions which come into play when rules are broken. Officially, all schools have broadly similar sanctions available to them. These range in a hierarchy from verbal rebukes and isolation within the classroom for minor offences to punishment exercises or detention for more serious offences and, ultimately, to suspension or exclusion from school. Minor offences are usually dealt with by the class teacher, while for the more serious offences, the schools' senior management become involved. The case-study schools used sanctions in rather different ways. How did the school's view of the pupil affect sanctions?

Detention

In Oldtown, pupil misbehaviour was not expected. When it did happen the school's main concern was that the use of sanctions should not disturb the work ethos. Sanctions were most often invoked within the individual class-room. Rule breaking which was sufficiently serious to be referred on by the head of department usually resulted in detention during breaks. This involved the pupil doing set work in the administration block, though out of sight of other pupils and of staff. The emphasis of the sanction was on the removal of the offender from the school's normal working pattern so that other pupils and staff could work unhindered. It was also important that the detention, while private and solitary, was work-oriented as dictated by the view of the pupil as scholar.

A contrasting way of using detention was evident at Braidburn. Instead of an academic work-oriented task out of sight of the rest of the school, offend-ers on detention usually found themselves with some socially useful task to carry out, for example picking up litter around the school. Another important difference was how the supervising teacher dealt with the offender. Often this was seen as an opportunity to get to know the pupil and, hopefully, to come to understand the reason for the bad behaviour. As one Braidburn teacher explained: 'Detention isn't just a punishment. It is a thing which helps us to get to know the pupils. [We] put them on jobs . . . you get a chat with them'.

Braidburn's view of the pupil as a member of the school community meant that the offender was punished in a way that benefited the community. Old-town's view of the pupil as scholar meant that the importance of work was reinforced within the use of the sanction. This indicated that the same sanctions/detention could be used quite differently depending on the view of the pupil held in the school.

In this section, we feel it is appropriate to discuss the use by one of our schools of a Pupil Support Unit (PSU). This may seem a contentious issue, as

official policy designates these as 'support' units encouraging positive behaviour. However, the use of this unit at Easthill suggested a sanction rather
than anything else. It was also described as a sanction by teachers interviewed.
The Easthill unit was described in the staff handbook as part of the overall
resources of the school there to provide ' . . . a strong support for both staff
and pupils . . . in order to enhance learning and discipline in the school'.

The unit was situated within the school and staffed by two full-time members of staff, and had the additional services of two educational psychologists
and a social worker. Within the unit were two rooms, divided by an interview
room. Room 1 was designated as a 'time-out' resource, where any pupil
requiring to be temporarily excluded from class could be sent. Transfer to
room 2 was a serious step, undertaken only after reintegration into mainstream schooling had failed and parents had been consulted.

It became clear during our time in this school that the aims of the unit staff
were quite severely at odds with those of mainstream staff. The PSU and its
staff encouraged positive behaviour by positively reinforcing good behaviour,
but this was very different from what was happening in the rest of the school.
The unit's positive reinforcement programme took several forms, many of
which involved incentives and treats unavailable to teachers and pupils in the
mainstream. For example: 'Quite a lot of our time is taken over by trips in the
form of rewards . . . also we have a points system, a kind of chart thing where
the children come in every day and we give them so many points'.

The problem was exacerbated, moreover, by a weakness in communication
between PSU staff and mainstream staff. Easthill teachers tended to use the
unit as a sanction when all other procedures, including punishment exercises
and referrals, had failed. Their doubts about the effectiveness of the unit were
clearly expressed in our interviews: 'Last year a boy was put to the unit . . . so
he gets his [subject taught] back here . . . it doesn't solve the problem – he's
not punished. It just moves [the problem] around'.

Here we encountered opposing views of the pupil within one school which
made the use of the PSU as an effective preventative measure virtually
impossible.

Once again, however, we see that these differences in applications bring
particular benefits and costs. What would be the benefit for a school such as
Oldtown which applied sanctions in a discreet way which did not disturb the
work of others? There would be a clear benefit in terms of allowing the
academic work of the school to proceed unhindered. There might also be
some benefit in levels of indiscipline being hidden, avoiding a 'copy cat' effect;
in other words, the school would be seen by pupils at large as having few
problems. This 'masking' of indiscipline, however, can also be a cost if staff
are not made aware of the number of detentions within the school.

In Braidburn, where sanctions were public, the benefits may be in terms of
the school being seen to act to protect the community when rules are broken.
A further benefit is that offenders are seen to be capable of correct behaviour
acceptable to the community. The obvious cost of this use of sanctions is in

the time and effort for staff involved. Perhaps less obvious is the cost of highlighting sanctions to such an extent that indiscipline in the school seems more prevalent than it is.

The above costs and benefits were clear to many of the teachers in our case-study schools. Whatever approach to sanctions is taken in any school, there will be costs and benefits. It is for schools to examine whether these are acceptable to them.

The behaviour card

The behaviour card is a document carried round by a pupil who has been in trouble and taken to each of his or her classes. At the end of each class the pupil has to have the card signed by the teacher, who also gives a mark for behaviour during the lesson and may add a written comment about this. This was the format for using the card, but how it was used in practice varied widely according to how the pupils were viewed. At St James and Braidburn the card was seen as a way of helping a 'reformed' pupil to maintain good standards of behaviour. In these schools the card was reserved for the pupils who were seen to have the potential to gain from using it. There was no suggestion that all misbehaving students be given such a card. It was issued sparingly and then only by the pastoral staff. In addition, it was important that parents were informed of the use of this card. A great deal of careful consideration therefore went into issuing the behaviour card at St James and Braidburn. Once it was issued, pastoral care staff in both schools spent time discussing the card with the pupil. Staff felt that it was important to involve the pupils in an assessment of their own behaviour, thus giving them a chance to understand why they behaved as they did. It also became clear that some pupils were given these as a means of supporting them against peer pressure to misbehave. One member of the pastoral care team at St James suggested that:

> I've got a boy just now . . . peer pressure in his class is so strong for truancy and poor behaviour that he needs the card for support. He told me he can turn to other pupils and say, 'I'm on a behaviour card check. I can't truant' . . . He's hiding behind the card, but it's giving him peace here.

The currency of the card was seen as high because its use was selective. Because it was used so sparingly its importance was clear to staff and pupils alike.

In Oldtown, the card was used in quite a different way. First, it was seen directly as a punishment for which there was little negotiation. Second, pupils were placed on behaviour cards not only by the pastoral care staff but also by subject teachers. This meant, in practice, that a pupil could be on several cards at the same time. It was possible, for example, for a pupil to be on a behaviour card issued by the English department, another issued by the mathematics department and a third by the pastoral care team. This obviously devalued the currency of the card. However, for Oldtown, this use was seen as appropriate because it fitted well with the view of the pupil as scholar. The card was used by the subject departments in order to fit the child to the particular work habits of that department. A typical comment on the aims of the behaviour card was that it should 'help the pupil become more efficient and to establish good work habits'.

Related to this was the absence of contact with parents over the use of the card. Whereas St James and Braidburn aimed to use the card in a comprehensive way, Oldtown was content to use it for problems which had been identified within a subject department and which would be dealt with there. This reflected the considerable autonomy of the department and the way that the school expected to take responsibility for the pupil as scholar.

The name of the sanction may be the same but the *way* these sanctions were used and, more importantly perhaps, their purposes, were different. The work ethic at Oldtown was reflected in the primacy of the subject departments, whose staff felt able to use their own behaviour cards for pupils to fit them for the work of that department. In contrast, at St James and Braidburn the work ethic was still important but only inasmuch as it was a *part* of the repertoire of the pupil in school. The purpose of the card at these schools was to try to alter behaviour by getting the child to recognise reasons for this behaviour over a number of subject areas. The emphasis was on rehabilitation or restoring the child to the school community in a supportive way. Once again, we see the way a particular disciplinary measure is used as reinforcing a school's view of its pupils.

As we emphasised in Chapter 1, it is not our intention to provide recipes for effective discipline either at whole school or classroom level. Schools have to operate in ways which seem most effective to them, given their particular contexts. What we can do is offer the schools concerned our speculations about the benefits and costs of their particular views of their pupils. It may be that these will strike chords with other schools and, if they are interested, provide a framework for re-examining how their view of pupils influences discipline.

The main benefits of Oldtown's approach were that there was an expectation of good behaviour, that the importance of work was self-evident and that time was not taken from the curriculum to discuss and debate rules. The rules were there to be obeyed implicitly and without argument. Their rationale and importance were taken for granted. The corresponding cost was that some pupils could fail to understand the values underlying the rules. This in turn could lead to some pupils feeling alienated from the school. As we shall see below, some teachers identified a 'them' and 'us' distinction being made by pupils who saw themselves as different from those they described as the 'snobs', pupils who were part of the school, and conformed to the school's values.

In Braidburn and St James the main benefit in explaining, debating and discussing rules and punishments was to encourage pupils to accept the schools' values and thereby come to accept the value of the curriculum on offer. Both schools were clear that only by this approach could they encourage good behaviour and academic endeavour on the part of their pupils. The costs were in terms of the time needed to ensure that rules were understood and in staff dealing with breaches of discipline.

Easthill's approach had the benefit of specifying clearly what the main rules were and the consequences if they were broken. The associated cost was the time spent in dealing with indiscipline because of the high number of rules broken. Because the system was essentially a reactive system, it was easy for it to become overloaded. Without clearly specified rules, however, the school might have degenerated into chaos.

Whether costs outweigh benefits or vice versa is for schools to judge, and degrees of each are obviously important. In Oldtown, for example, the possible alienation of a small number of pupils might well be a price worth paying for the solid academic achievement of the majority. If the number of disaffected pupils increased then the cost might be too great. Similarly, if the time needed to make pupils feel part of the school community made serious inroads into the time available for the academic curriculum, no doubt St James and Braidburn would want to reconsider their approach.

So far we have been considering how its view of its pupils affects what the school counts as good discipline and how it reacts to indiscipline. We now turn to the influence of the view of the pupil on the promotion of good discipline. We consider this under two main headings, the kinds of incentives towards and rewards for good discipline and the role of the pastoral care system.

Incentives and rewards for good discipline

It is well documented that teachers as a group are not much given to praising and rewarding pupils. Perhaps not surprisingly, therefore, teachers found it easier to talk about school systems for reacting to indiscipline than to identify specific incentives for promoting discipline. This may also partly be because incentives towards good behaviour are amorphous and are associated with the curriculum provided and the expectations set, rather than with specific rewards. However, we were able to identify different kinds of incentives used in the four case-study schools. These included a prefect system, pupil councils, assemblies, prize-givings and merit systems. We would argue that the school's view of its pupils influenced not only the kind of incentives used but the way they were used.

One of the incentives used in St James to promote good behaviour among year one and year two pupils was a merit league. Each class was awarded points for good work and good behaviour from each subject teacher. The class with the highest score was given a treat, such as a class party, or a school trip. It was interesting to us that it was *group* behaviour which was the focus of attention, which would seem to emphasise the view of pupils as members of a community. This contrasts with prize-giving in Oldtown where the reward was largely for individual endeavour in academic or sporting achievement. The pupil as scholar was being rewarded.

Both Oldtown and Braidburn had prefects – senior pupils in years five and six who had stayed on at school beyond the statutory leaving age. In both schools the prefects played a similar role. They carried out some supervisory duties, organised charity work and acted as a filter of views between pupils and senior management staff. In Oldtown the prefects were selected by the teaching staff, with the headteacher having final power over the selection. They seemed to be chosen to represent the value the school placed on scholarly success. They tended to be the most academically successful pupils. It was inconceivable, for example, that the school 'dux' (the most able scholar) would not be a prefect. The prefects were seen as providing an aspirational model for the younger pupils. In Braidburn, on the other hand, the prefects were chosen by the pupils. We would suggest that this is further evidence of the community ethos which the school sought to convey. Two comments from senior staff talking about the prefect system highlight the differences in approach. The first is from the Assistant Headteacher at Oldtown, the second from the Assistant Headteacher at Braidburn:

[The prefect system] gives them [the prefects] a sense of belonging – a say in the affairs [of the school] – and it makes it easier for us to get them to do what we want them to do.

I think the prefects are becoming much more of a representative body for the pupils, rather than for enforcing school rules.

Our observation notes and information from pupils suggested that there had been some confrontation between pupils and prefects at Oldtown as they went about their supervisory duties. This happened less frequently at Braidburn, perhaps because the prefects adopted a less supervisory role or perhaps because they had been elected rather than selected.

In speculating about the benefits and costs of incentive systems we should recognise that giving rewards may have unintended effects. The merit system in St James worked in that most classes strove to win. However, it did emphasise competition which the school saw as acceptable if all classes had a chance of winning. Staff remarked that some classes apparently set up an unofficial competition to find the worst behaved class!

Prefect systems have their benefits and costs too. They are intended to provide some pupils with the opportunity of influencing school affairs and of accepting wider responsibilities. Not everyone can be a prefect and so the possibilities of division exist. Some teachers in Oldtown, particularly those involved in guidance and learning support, saw potential for a 'them' and 'us' situation developing among pupils. The Learning Support teacher who saw many of the disenfranchised and disenchanted pupils at Oldtown commented: 'I don't feel the pupils all feel they belong to the same school. There's a 'them' and 'us' . . . My kids call the others 'snobs'. The fifth and sixth years go to plays but there's not much for the kids that I see . . . they are not interested in [non-academic pupils]'.

Perhaps the most important point to make is the absence of clear incentives for good behaviour. Maybe it is part of our culture. We are not rewarded for doing what we ought; we are punished if we transgress. We wonder if rewards for teachers and for pupils could form a more integral part of school practice.

Pastoral care

Virtually all Scottish secondary schools have guidance staff who have responsibilities for pastoral care. In most schools these staff provide a social education curriculum for pupils and offer individual counselling to pupils needing help and support. Pastoral staff are also subject specialists and have teaching duties in their subject specialism. Most schools designate a member of the senior management team as having a particular responsibility for pastoral care.

In all four case-study schools, pastoral care was organised in similar ways. Each pastoral care teacher had a number of pupils allocated on a vertical system. This meant that their case-load involved pupils from year one through to year six. A year one pupil would, therefore, have the same pastoral teacher throughout his or her school career. Over and above this, there were 'year heads', who were responsible for years one to two, three to four and five to six. These year heads were usually appointed from the senior management team. Once again, however, apparently similar systems operated in rather different ways.

In Braidburn, the aim of the pastoral system was set out in the brochure. The emphasis was on the pupil as a person, a member of the school community:

> Pastoral staff aim to help the pupils with any problem they have relating to . . . school; settling in, relationships with other pupils and with staff, behavioural problems, subject and course choices, careers advice and personal problems. If outwith school, problems come to our notice, we would wish to discuss these as well.

Here the school is conveying its concern about academic progress but places these among wider ranging concerns about the pupils' social and personal development.

In Oldtown, the brochure emphasised the role of pastoral staff in assisting the pupil's development as scholar:

> Guidance teachers are involved in:
> 1 introducing the pupils to the school and house system, issuing them with their timetable and explaining aspects of school organisation concerning the courses available, facilities for social and recreational activities and recreational activities outwith the curriculum.
> 2 monitoring and maintaining records of pupils' attendance, their academic progress and matters related to their welfare in the school.
> 3 supplying teaching staff with information that will assist them in providing appropriate courses for pupils.

Of course, Oldtown was also interested in the social welfare of pupils. However, the emphasis on this is less pronounced than in Braidburn. Once again it is all a matter of degree, but subtle degrees of emphasis can have important effects on discipline policy and practice. These differing emphases in policy statements about the role of guidance were also carried through in practice.

In Oldtown, the taken-for-granted nature of pupils' social and personal skills meant that there was no apparent need for a social education programme. Parents were providing all the social education necessary. A programme had been tried in the school in the past and had not been viewed favourably by staff. The role of pastoral staff was to offer advice on subject choice and careers, which they did through a programme of interviews with all pupils, and to help pupils with problems outside the scope of subject teachers.

At Braidburn, where pupils' personal and social development was not taken for granted, pastoral staff played a major role in developing and teaching a social education programme. This programme covered discussion on topics such as health education, stereotyping and problems of adolescence. In addition, all pupils were interviewed annually by guidance staff for personal, curricular or vocational guidance. In practice, therefore, all pupils were likely to discuss a variety of matters with guidance staff either in class or individually. In Oldtown, pupils who did not have particular problems were likely to see pastoral staff only on curricular or vocational matters.

What were the benefits and costs of these contrasting approaches? Oldtown operated on the assumption that a social education programme was unnecessary because most of its pupils came from home backgrounds which provided the same values as the school. The absence of a social education programme undoubtedly provided more time for other curriculum activities. The cost is the one already identified by research studies. It is argued that without such a programme schools depend on children demonstrating problems before they can act. What if a child does not demonstrate experiencing a problem? The assumption is all is well. A further cost is that a system which caters only for 'problem' children can produce labelling. Such children are denied the high status accorded to the conventionally successful. They may then seek alternative status through deviance which can be manifested as problem behaviour. The 'them' and 'us' comments made by staff at Oldtown were early indications of this process.

The cost to St James and Braidburn of their extensive pastoral care provision was the time and other resources involved. The benefits were in terms of positive contributions to the pupils' social and emotional development. The consensus at both schools was that benefits outweighed costs. As one Braidburn teacher summed up: 'It's a more demanding and gradual process [social education] but, in the end *with these kids* [our emphasis] it's a better one'.

The important point for us to stress is that pastoral care policy and the role played by pastoral staff were influenced by the school's view of its pupils.

Were pupils aware of their schools' views?

So far we have concentrated on describing what we have called the school's view of its pupils. We have argued that there is a dominant view and have shown how this affects whole school discipline policy and practice. Were the pupils aware that the school held a particular view of them? This seemed to us to be an important question to ask for two reasons. First, it seemed to be a matter of plain common sense that for a particular view to have an impact on the way the pupils behaved, pupils would need to be aware of it. It would be no good emphasising the importance of particular values and codes of conduct at staff level if these were never communicated to the pupils. Second, pupils' views on their schools' discipline policies and practices would help to validate what we have presented as the schools' views. In each of the four schools we asked pupils to write about the school rules which affected them most and to say why they affected them. We collected views from 567 pupils in years one to four, which gave us some valuable insights into the salience for them of particular rules.

Initially, we found a good deal of commonality among pupils across the four schools. This was hardly surprising when we considered that they had answered the question, 'Which school rule affects you most?'. This question had been chosen to identify the operational day-to-day rules from the pupils' perspective. If the pupils had been asked to hypothesise as to which rule was most important in the school, a quite different response might have been given. It was to be expected, therefore, that pupils mentioned rules which affected them directly.

However, what was probably more revealing than quantification of the pupil response was its tone. At Easthill, for example, where pupils were viewed in deficit terms, most of the pupils described the rules in restrictive and negative terms, echoing the school brochure. For example: 'Not allowed to talk in the classroom'. 'Not allowed to sit in the cloakrooms'. 'You have to do your work or else you get a punishment exercise'.

That is not to say that pupils in the other schools did not also mention restrictive rules. The rule on school uniform was seen as particularly restrictive. There seemed, however, to be more of an awareness of the rationality of the rules. At St James, for example, this year three girl gave the rules in the following way: 'No running in corridors – this affects us because accidents can happen if you run and we could be involved in them'. 'Make sure no valuables are left in the changing rooms because if they are stolen you are held responsible'.

We could speculate that the social education programme at St James, where lessons were devoted to discussing the rationale for rules had paid dividends.

When asked about the results of rule-breaking, pupils also seemed to understand how the school regarded them. For example, pupils were asked to consider a time when a rule was broken, to describe what happened and to say whether things worked out well. In Braidburn and St James, where pupils were regarded as part of the community and family, rules had to be seen as for the benefit of everyone. Much of the response from the pupils at those two schools reflected this. At Braidburn, for example, several pupils described incidents where windows were accidentally broken by groups of boys playing football. One of the boys described such an incident as follows: 'In the playground, when you are playing football, if you break a window everybody who is playing is punished. They [teachers] find the cost of the window and split it [the cost] evenly between each player'. The pupil goes on to suggest that this is a successful resolution of the problem because 'It is not just the person who kicked the ball that pays – so when someone wants to play near the window everybody else says "No".'

At Easthill, the pupils' responses had much more to do with the re-calcitrant pupil 'deserving the punishment' and less to do with recognition of the value of the rule. For example, a year two pupil relating an incident of a pupil fight in the school corridor describes how things turned out well because the perpetrator was 'sent away from school and won't bother that person who he battered'. The Easthill pupils appeared in subtle ways to be aware of the school's view that the rules were necessary to make up for the deficiencies of the pupils.

Conclusion

In this chapter we have tried to show that though schools operated along similar lines, they held distinctive views of their pupils and that these views affected discipline policy and practice.

As we mentioned at the beginning of the chapter, two of the schools, Easthill and St James, had large numbers of pupils from areas high in indices of social deprivation. Oldtown took pupils largely from a prosperous middle-class catchment area and Braidburn was the only school serving a small, relatively homogeneous town. Two of the schools, St James and Braidburn, viewed their pupils in broadly similar ways. They were to be welcomed into an environment where they were valued, where great efforts were made to explain the rationale for rules and, crucially, where they were involved in promoting and maintaining discipline. This approach, we argue, is strongly associated with a view of pupils as members of the school family or community. Bad behaviour by any one pupil had effects on this communi-ty as a whole and so efforts had to be made to understand such behaviour and to work co-operatively to prevent it happening again. Similarly, 'good' behaviour by a group was rewarded through the merit system.

In Oldtown and Easthill we would argue that the approach was one of telling the pupils to conform to the schools' values. In Oldtown this was reasonably straightforward because of the good catchment area. Bad be-haviour was not expected and indeed did not often occur. In Easthill, bad behaviour was expected because of the nature of the catchment area and a system of rules and punishments was clearly spelt out. This was in place to protect the teachers and well-behaved pupils against the likelihood of disruptive behaviour by a large minority.

What do other studies of discipline have to tell us about the kinds of systems reported in this chapter? First of all, studies by Hargreaves (1967) and Egglestone (1979) suggest that schools do indeed label pupils and that pupils pick up *coded* messages from teachers about their perceived worth. Our data reinforce this view. Second, Reynolds and Sullivan (1979) found in their study of secondary modern schools in South Wales that schools which tried to involve pupils in the life of the school were more successful in academic terms and in terms of pupil behaviour. They also concluded that coercive schools which were rigid in their discipline were less successful because they underestimated their pupils' abilities and upbringing. Here our data are less clear. Measures of academic success and indiscipline are contentious and the available data do not allow us to make direct comparisons across the four schools. What the Reynolds and Sullivan research does provide is a rationale for St James and Braidburn adopting the approach they did. Although Oldtown held a dominant view of the pupil as scholar this did not mean that no effort was made to involve pupils in the life of the school. Differences between these three schools were a matter of degree. As we have emphasised, throughout, however, there are no simple recipes and no right or wrong answers for discipline policy. Each school's view of its pupils had benefits and costs and we summarise these in Table 2.1 below. We should explain that the table is not a summary of what we have described in each of the case-study schools; the ideas contained are intended to reflect the inherent benefits and costs from taking these particular views of pupils. They are certainly not seen as an exhaustive list and readers may be able to suggest alternatives.

Table 2.1:   Benefits and costs: Schools view their pupils in particular and distinctive ways and these views affect discipline policy and practice

Pupil as scholar	Pupil as community/family	Pupil as socially deficient
HOW RULES ARE APPLIED		
Most rules are conveyed formally and are copied out by the pupils. Rules of social behaviour are taken for granted.	Rules are conveyed formally. Rules are also explained and discussed through the social education programme.	Rules are prescriptive and extensive and are applied reactively, ie when a pupil breaks a rule.
Benefits • Pupils have access to clear rules.	*Benefits* • Pupils understand the rationale of the rules.	*Benefits* • The rules and their consequences are spelled out clearly.
Costs • Some pupils fail to understand the value/ relevance of the rules.	*Costs* • Time allocated for discussion of the rules limits time available for other areas of the curriculum.	*Costs* • The rule system becomes overloaded.

HOW SANCTIONS ARE APPLIED

Sanctions should not disrupt the work of others.

Sanctions have to be recognised by the community. Some sanctions may have a community value, eg litter collection.

Sanctions have to be applied promptly and unequivocally.

Benefits
- Work of the school goes on unhindered.
- Less visible use of sanctions masks the levels of indiscipline.

Benefits
- Staff in the school are seen to act to protect the community when rules are broken.
- Sanctions are seen as having a rehabilitative effect.

Benefits
- Pupils know what to expect.

Costs
- The deterrent effect of the punishment is not obvious to other pupils.
- Indiscipline will be less visible when privately punished.

Costs
- More visible use of sanctions highlights the levels of indiscipline.

Costs
- The use of sanctions is time consuming for staff.
- Dealing with indiscipline may become more important than work.

HOW PUPILS ARE REWARDED

Rewards are mainly for academic behaviour.

Rewards are geared towards cooperation/group cohesion.

Rewards have to do with negotiating the amount of work to be done.

Benefits
- Work is seen as valued.

Benefits
- Group cooperation is seen to be valued. Pupils are predisposed towards group discipline.

Benefits
- The teacher is given scope to determine the balance between work and rewards.

Costs
- Some children are never rewarded.
- There is a danger of polarisation of pupils into those rewarded by system and those who are not.

Costs
- Work is not as highly valued as cooperation/group cohesion.
- For some pupils group cohesion is directed to bad behaviour.

Costs
- Work is devalued in the eyes of the pupils when less work is a reward.

HOW PASTORAL CARE OPERATES

The subject departments are seen as the first resource in advising most of the pupils.

Pastoral care is seen as a support network for both pupils and teachers.

Pastoral care is seen as relieving pressure on teachers – reactive and fire fighting.

Benefits
- Pastoral care is able to concentrate on the minority of pupils, those with problems.

Benefits
- Pupils and teachers feel confident that pastoral care is helping to promote whole school discipline.

Benefits
- This allows teachers a respite from individual pupil's behaviour.

Costs
- Pastoral care is for pupils with problems.
- The need for a social education programme is not recognised by subject teachers.

Costs
- Time and resources will have to be diverted from subject work to produce an effective pastoral care programme.

Costs
- Teachers feel that guidance intervention has only a short-term effect.
- Resources available for a general social education programme are depleted.
- Pastoral care will become overloaded.

Examining your school's view of its pupils

1 What messages about pupils does your school convey through:
   - the school brochure
   - the system of rules and sanctions
   - rewards, if any, for good behaviour
   - the way the pastoral care system works?
2 Check your interpretation of the message with a variety of staff. It may be that people who don't agree with the view will have useful things to say. Remember, this is what happened in our research.
3 Are these intended messages? If not, what can you do to make sure the intended message gets across?
4 What do you see as the main benefits and costs of your current system? Check the table, identify the areas of match and mismatch for your own school. What are the implications of these?
5 Where can improvements be made? What will the benefits be? Will they outweigh costs? The table gives some examples of likely costs and benefits of different approaches.

References

Egglestone, J. (1979) The construction of deviance in school, in L. Barton, and R. Meighan, (eds.) *Schools, Pupils and Deviance*, Nafferton Books, Nafferton.

Hargreaves, D. H. (1967) *Social Relations in a Secondary School*, Routledge & Kegan Paul, London.

Hargreaves, D. H. (1976) Reactions to labelling, in M. Hammersley, and P. Woods, (eds.) *The Process of Schooling*, Routledge & Kegan Paul/Open University Press, London.

Reynolds, D. and Sullivan, M. (1979) Bringing schools back in, in L. Barton, and R. Meighan, (eds.) *Schools, Pupils and Deviance*, Nafferton Books, Nafferton.

3

THE TEACHERS' VIEW OF TEACHING

In this chapter we look at how a school's view of its pupils can affect the teachers and how the teachers translate this into particular actions related to classroom and school discipline. We believe from our case-study materials that how a school sees its pupils affects the behavioural goals which teachers see as realistic and achievable. The key idea here, therefore, is that: *teachers' views of the main purpose of teaching influence classroom discipline. These purposes are, in turn, influenced by the school's view of its pupils.*

Certain broad aims in terms of the purposes of teaching are proclaimed by all teachers. These can be summed up as pupils learning what it is intended they should learn and developing each child to his or her full potential. However, as any teacher knows, these broad aims are influenced by a whole range of conditions, not least of which is the attitude of the pupil. How often has the new teacher arrived in school brimming over with idealism and enthusiasm to teach his or her subject, awaken an interest in pupils and develop a keenness for learning, only to be confronted with the cold reality of a classroom where apathy and indifference can escalate into disorder. New teachers find quickly that teaching does not take place in a vacuum. They also find that their views about teaching may have to be modified according to the prevailing conditions in the school. Research into the transition of teachers from college to school suggests that probationary teachers quickly take on board the established mores of the school. The pressure to conform to school traditions is very strong. Little is known about how this influence works, although research on the socialisation of teachers gives us some clues. The staff-room, for example, is often a place where problems can be admitted and shared, and, in the process, reinforce the school's view of its pupils. Similarly, subject department work bases can provide a similar function in establishing an accepted subject tradition.

We begin with a broad picture of what all teachers interviewed said about school discipline within their own schools. Then we will go on to look at what our four observed teachers in each school said about classroom discipline. (This later section is also taken up and examined more closely in Chapters 6 and 7.)

There were some quite striking differences about the way staff communicated with one another in our four schools, as Chapter 5 explains. Social contact among staff at Oldtown was generally restricted to certain groupings. Teachers with the same outlook on teaching, and often from the same department, tended to sit together at coffee and lunch breaks. Particular departments or groups were associated with particular staff-rooms. In Oldtown, there were three staff-rooms, 'ladies', 'gentlemen' and 'mixed' and so staff tended to meet in departmental sub-sets in different rooms. As a result, communication among teachers from different departments required more of an effort. Of course, teacher friendships cut across departments, but the tendency was towards clearly defined groupings based on similar views of teaching.

In Braidburn and St James, the staff met regularly in a general staff-room and there was a great deal more communication between departments. Cliques were not apparent or were more difficult to identify. At St James, staff from all departments sat together and views were openly shared and, indeed, vigorously debated. Pupils and discipline were accepted topics of conversation both within and across departments. There was obviously much less of a departmental view at these schools than at Oldtown.

At Easthill, staff tended to communicate with their own departments. It seemed that this was only partially due to the physical constraints of the building and more to do with attempting to establish a strong departmental rationale to enforce discipline in the school. In other words, it was easier for staff to communicate their concerns to colleagues in their own area who understood these specific problems than to a range of staff in other departments.

We would not wish to claim too much for these differences, as we were present in the schools for a relatively short time and groups may well have been in operation in subtle ways. All we can say is that, superficially, the contrast between Oldtown and Easthill on the one hand and St James and Braidburn on the other, was quite striking. Our intention is to describe the transformation of the teachers' views of their pupils into goals which were seen as realistic and achievable, and then consider what this means for classroom discipline, rather than to discuss the socialisation of teachers.

The main sources of evidence for teachers' goals and the implications for classroom discipline were interviews with teachers whose lessons we observed and with a range of other staff in the schools. Teachers talked at length about what they wanted pupils to achieve and how particular actions were more appropriate than others in getting these goals implemented. They also described a range of conditions which they suggested affected whether certain goals were feasible.

How do teachers translate the school view into classroom practice?

Teachers in all four schools talked about encouraging the pupils to learn by using a variety of actions. These included choosing an appropriate curriculum, pacing the material and attempting to establish good relationships with pupils. However, as we shall illustrate, the emphases differed among the schools.

The academic curriculum leading towards the public examination system was the main focus of teaching in Oldtown. The teachers held a view of teaching which involved the transmission of a set body of knowledge necessary for success in public examinations. The emphasis was on the teachers telling pupils about selected items which they felt were relevant. There was a feeling of contractual understanding between pupils and teachers, that both had a job to do. The teacher's part of the contract was to be well-prepared and to present the material in an interesting and acceptable form. The pupils' part was to accept the material and apply themselves to internalising it. Underpinning this view of teaching and learning was a taken-for-granted notion of pupils at Oldtown who were well motivated to learn. As one Oldtown teacher explained: 'Pupils are here to learn . . . That's the long and short of it really . . . Behaviour which is irrelevant to the working pattern just should not happen. Generally, though we have no trouble . . . pupils know what they are here for'. We can see here how Oldtown's view of its pupils as scholars is transformed into work-related goals and into a classroom discipline which is concerned with pupils getting on with academic work.

In Braidburn, there was more emphasis on the need to motivate pupils to learn. The school wanted pupils to feel part of a community and realised that the local culture was not one where the academic curriculum was highly valued. Pupils had to be persuaded of its value and this was translated into particular teaching goals highlighting the need to interest pupils in their academic work. It was also important to cater for a wide ability range, as teachers felt that pupils who could not cope with the work would be 'turned off' and more likely to cause disruption within the classroom. Braidburn pupils, in general, were 'biddable' but not academically well motivated; they had to be encouraged. As one Braidburn teacher said: 'The teacher's got to be there as a guiding force . . . [Pupils] need to be kept active, they need to be kept involved . . . I think in our phrase, "you gotta zing it to them" . . . I've got a responsibility to them to make it come alive'.

There was little in this school's view of its pupils which assumed they would learn without this 'zing'. The teachers felt that this was necessary and that it was their responsibility to provide it.

At St James, the school view of its pupils was similar to that of Braidburn. Likewise, therefore, goals emphasised teaching for understanding and relevance. Pupils were thought to lack confidence and self-esteem, particularly in academic subjects, so the encouragement of pupils was a high priority for teachers at this school. A relevant curriculum was seen as essential and this was interpreted widely. Though the traditional academic syllabus and the public examination system were important, the understanding of concepts and relating this to pupils' real lives appeared to us to be a more salient goal for staff at St James: 'Successful learning has to do with interest, attempting to make it interesting and stimulating. You can't always achieve that, some bits are very dry and difficult for them, but you try to keep it concrete'.

The view of teaching at Braidburn and St James involved motivating pupils sufficiently so that they were able to learn.

Easthill's dominant teaching goals concerned getting through the syllabus with a minimum of confrontation. As at Oldtown, the emphasis was on telling or transmitting knowledge from teacher to pupil. Their view of teaching was strongly affected by the school's view of the pupil as deficient in many social skills as well as academic motivation. It was further influenced by the high rate of absenteeism at the school which made teaching in a continuous and consolidating way very difficult indeed. There was a contractual or even bargaining aspect to Easthill's view of teaching. Teachers would negotiate how much work the pupil was required to do in exchange for minimal disruption of the lesson.

One example of pupils' low motivation was the difficulty staff found in having homework completed. A number of pupils regularly failed to complete homework assignments and teachers found that enforcing this rule had become untenable. The following quotation may give an idea of the problem:

> If homework isn't done, they have to report to [Assistant Headteacher (AHT)] . . . but there's no sanction we can use really to get it done. It's difficult to enforce a homework policy when the kids see that others are getting away with not doing it . . . so it's now abandoned. It's not worth the hassle . . . trying to get them all to do the homework . . .

Staff felt that confrontation with pupils was to be avoided if at all possible and negotiation of certain basic work standards was preferred. This bargaining aspect is reflected below:

> We have to do it [school work] within a set number of written rules – and let's get on with it. But I will make it as pleasant as possible for you and I will not ask you to do anything unreasonable – and so let's get on with it.

A culinary metaphor might help to clarify the differences between the schools. The menu and the implements for eating were the same at Oldtown and at Easthill. The difference was that there were quite different appetites. At Braidburn and St James the staff ensured that their clients were hungry enough to enjoy the meal by providing the appropriate aperitifs.

Of course, as well as teaching goals, staff had other goals for their pupils which had to do with social skills. Teachers' views in our case-study schools of what their contribution should be were very much influenced by how they saw the pupils. For example, at Oldtown where pupils were seen as coming from homes where positive social skills were taken for granted, teachers did not feel that their contribution should be a major one. A typical comment regarding social expectations was: 'I would expect every person who comes from a reasonable home has had instilled in them a general sense of how they should behave. . .'

It was taken for granted that pupils would behave in a particular way and those who did not were seen as 'beyond the pale' by some teachers and treated accordingly. Pupils who lacked the expected social skills or who rebelled against the school's expectations were viewed as 'less able' and provided with an 'appropriate curriculum' which tended as often as not to be 'non-academic'.

At Easthill, in contrast, poor social training from parents was assumed and teachers felt that this was so difficult a case that they were uneasy about tackling it. The job of instilling basic social training was such an onerous one that they allowed few classroom occasions where disruption could occur. Pupils were contained within a traditional teacher-directed environment which allowed for little pupil participation. Participation was seen as liable to produce troublesome behaviour. A typical comment reflecting this view was:

> There are things you'd like to do with pupils like these – like debates and discussion
> – and sometimes you do try it . . . but likely as not they go right over the score and
> you've got chaos. Now, no one wants that – not even the kids . . . so we don't do
> much of that here.

In contrast, at St James, pupils' social training was given a high priority by the teaching staff. Though pupils were seen as having certain social problems, these were problems which St James teachers felt willing and able to deal with. Perhaps because of the common Catholic background or their particular professional viewpoint, pupils were seen as part of the school family. Staff suggested that it was their responsibility to inculcate acceptable values to those pupils through the school curriculum. In addition, the headteacher held strongly to the notion that schools can and do make a difference. Also, social training at St James was seen as going hand in hand with intellectual training. To take one example, the use of problem-solving as an approach was deemed to be useful for academic as well as social reasons. As mentioned in Chapter 1, both St James and Easthill took children from catchment areas with a wide variety of social problems. Why then did St James react in one way to their social training and Easthill in another? We have no clear evidence on this and can only speculate. However, it seems that the purpose of teaching is heavily influenced by how the school views its pupils. While Easthill viewed its pupils as socially deficient, St James, despite evidence to the contrary, refused to accept this view. St James pupils were a part of the school community, however bleak and deprived their home background. This was an extremely idealistic, some might say naïve view to take, but it was one which was adopted by the school, led by a school management team and reinforced by a consensus of teacher attitudes throughout the school. The effect of positive and negative labelling of pupils has to be an underlying factor when looking at the teachers' views of teaching in these two seemingly similar, but essentially contrasting, schools.

Teachers' goals and classroom discipline

Each of our case-study schools appeared to take a different view of the purposes of teaching. Some of these purposes contrasted quite sharply while others were more subtle, and in this section we discuss their influence on classroom discipline. Before describing this, however, it is necessary to say a little about how we collected our information.

In each school we studied four teachers who had been identified by pupils as effective at 'getting the class to work well'. We observed the teachers with two different classes over a fortnight, and as near as possible to the observed lesson we asked, 'What did you do to get the class to work well?' We were interested in the teachers' own views of what they did rather than in comparing their view with ours. In addition to describing their actions, teachers talked more specifically about what they meant by getting the class to work well. It is largely from these statements that we have built up what we have called their view of teaching. In analysing our data it seemed to us that there were close associations with the school's view of its pupils. There were strong patterns among the four teachers in each school which overrode subject differences. We cannot claim too much, given our research approach. All we can do is to suggest that the school's view of its pupils impinged on classroom discipline. These suggestions were reinforced by our data from a wider sample of teachers on more general matters about whole school, subject department and classroom discipline. (A fuller consideration of teachers' classroom discipline is contained in Chapters 6 and 7.)

In Easthill, working well at classroom level was described largely in terms of keeping pupils busy. Teachers tried to make sure the pupils had enough to do and that their attention was held. We might infer that this lessened opportunities for disruption. We argue in Chapter 6 that teacher purposes or goals are affected by the conditions operating in the classroom. Perhaps one of the most salient conditions for the teacher at Easthill was the presence of poorly motivated pupils who were likely to disrupt the lesson at any given opportunity. Easthill teachers' goals were also affected by their experience of how difficult it was to achieve academic success, given not only the low motivation of pupils but also the high absentee rate. If, for example, a teacher aimed to develop in the pupil an understanding of a particular concept over a period of weeks, this aim was often thwarted when the attendance rates of individual pupils were so erratic. As one teacher from Easthill explained: 'You have great hopes when you come in. Some of these kids are quite interested . . . Then you find that you haven't seen a pupil for several weeks . . . it's very demoralising for a teacher . . .'

Many of the teachers at Easthill reflected this view and gave examples of the conditions which led to teacher demoralisation and of having to adopt a fall-back position of teaching as containment. In other words, their aim had to be adapted to that of keeping pupils busy and occupied and it was clear that conditions within the school had steadily influenced this outlook.

In contrast, the goals identified by the teachers at St James tended to be cognitive and affective. Typical of goals were 'to involve them [pupils] so that they can see the relevance of science to everyday life', and to 'try to make it concrete . . . it is about trying to bring abstract thoughts to a concrete level'. These fitted well with the school's stress on the understanding of concepts, the motivation of pupils and the pupil-centred notion of its philosophy.

The purposes of teaching at Oldtown concentrated on transmitting an agreed body of knowledge through a traditionally structured curriculum. The goals which were important involved a contractual relationship made up of the teacher instructing and the child listening and absorbing. For example: 'I tried to find out who knew what . . . you have to have the attention of the class before you start to teach so that they get the point of the lesson'.

Of course, there were important conditions impinging on the teachers at Oldtown which had led them to view teaching in this way. One of the most crucial was the pressure on teachers for pupils to achieve, pressure brought to bear by parents and perhaps, indeed, by the pupils themselves. The school was seen as one where academic merit was highly prized. This most prominent aim of the school affected what teachers saw as classes working well.

What we have described so far are the different conditions in these four schools as outlined by the teachers we observed (Chapter 6 outlines our analysis in more detail). Though we would have to say that four teachers cannot claim to represent the views of all the teachers in these schools, there was sufficient similarity among them for us to claim that there was an overall consensus on the conditions affecting what teachers felt they were able to do. As Chapter 6 more fully illustrates, the most frequently mentioned condition was what teachers described as 'knowledge of the child'. This involved knowledge about the pupil's home background and his or her ability and behaviour in previous lessons. How teachers interpreted this knowledge and how this affected what they should do to attain their goals were aspects crucial to their view of teaching. For example, if teachers felt that conditions were so negatively constraining, they would often limit the goals which they set for pupils.

When teachers at Oldtown described their knowledge of the pupil as that of an academic recipient, they were likely to also describe a goal which involved academic transmission. Similarly, when Easthill teachers described pupils who were poorly motivated, academically limited, and whose attendance was often erratic, their goals were expressed in terms of getting through the work with the minimum of disruption. The actions they chose to attain their goals are described in the next section.

Teachers' actions

After observing what each of our case study teachers did, we asked them to tell us in their own words what they did to get the class to work well. We later examined their discourse and found different patterns associated with each of the schools.

In Easthill, our four teachers talked predominantly about such actions as 'verbal rebukes' or 'using sanctions' to maintain discipline. Some 33 per cent of all the actions mentioned by the four teachers fell into these categories. In St James, where the catchment area was similar, 19 per cent of the actions mentioned by the four teachers fell into these categories. This is not a criticism of either school but is suggestive of the influence which the school's view of its pupils can have on classroom practice. Let us take an example. A science teacher at Easthill described the following lesson. He stressed the importance of setting up an attitude conducive to learning and teaching as pupils do not bring this attitude to school:

> First of all make sure that you are here before they are . . . you must be here otherwise they go off at all sorts of strange tangents. Make sure they get their books out straight away and jackets off. Don't allow them to do anything else until that has been done . . . it gives them the idea that they have to do some work that period . . . I'm continually making sure that they get the idea that if I'm saying something it's important and keep the concentration until after I'm finished . . . and getting in amongst them checking that they are getting on with the writing they've been asked to do. If you don't *check* it, there's no point in doing it.

This teacher felt that pupils required to be watched continually, otherwise inattention and disruption would ensue. He was concerned that pupils spend their time productively, and continually monitored their behaviour to ensure that this happened. The point to be made is that the teacher, because of his knowledge of the class, felt that his teaching strategy had to involve a great deal of monitoring of the pupils' behaviour. Explaining and helping actions could only be effective after he had ensured that disruptive behaviour had ceased.

In contrast, a teacher at St James describes the following lesson, the success of which is determined by interest and engagement with the material:

> They're working because they're all engaged . . . Rather than getting a pupil to sit down and copy – and pupils are quite happy to do that – I don't allow that, it's not educational – all it is is keeping them quiet and occupied . . . They must develop the skill to describe the practical work in their own words and [eventually] they do it quite well . . . the English may not be great, but as long as they are understanding what they are doing, that's as much as I'm after . . .

The difference between the two situations described is that the first teacher has both a taken-for-granted notion of pupils as deficient and a view of teaching which accords with this – one which concerns keeping pupils busy, occupied and less likely to cause trouble. The actions used have to do with checking and monitoring pupil behaviour to avert disruption. The second situation accords with the view of the pupil and of teaching at St James which is based on motivating pupils to learn for understanding. While teachers at Easthill working in a difficult context felt that classroom work had to be closely watched and teacher directed, the St James teachers felt that by working within a supportive framework they were freed to engage much more with pupils. Teachers at St James outlined a view of teaching which stressed teacher and pupil working together towards increasing an understanding of the subject.

Even where teachers talk about using the *same action* to maintain class-room discipline, the school's view of its pupils influences what counts as good discipline. For example, the action of 'going round the class' at St James has a subtly different purpose from that suggested at Easthill:

> [I was] going round the class, looking at pupil work, discussing pupil work, discussing results with them, showing them [by] my interest that I want them to get a good result for a particular experiment and then I'm involved with them in the practical work . . .
>
> (Teacher, St James)

> I try to get round . . . it's a small class and quite easy to get round. It helps because they know you are going to come round – and if you've come up 5 minutes ago and they are still on the same question and you say, 'What's happening, then?' and one of the answers here to that is, 'Oh I'm stuck' and you say, 'Why is your hand not up then? That's a lot of nonsense'. You can sort of turn it back on them . . . But if you're coming round to check their work, it encourages them to keep going. If you are divorced from them for the whole period they can sit and do nothing.
>
> (Teacher, Easthill)

What we have described, using Easthill and St James, are two similar actions taken for two different purposes. These teachers' views of teaching influenced what happened in the classrooms. Our other case-study schools also had distinctive views about what teaching was for and these, too, influenced the teachers' classroom behaviour and what they counted for their classes as working well.

This meant in practice that the teachers' goals at each of the four schools set the agenda for what happened in the classroom. An Oldtown teacher described a lesson which he felt had worked well in the following way:

> It went very well. The children were well behaved. It was a new room and there was nothing on the walls. [The material] had been taken down for the exams [so that there were no distractions]. Also it was a difficult topic, difficult to get across. The more able were managing, although they did have some difficulties . . . Again, they were well behaved, it's a pattern for years one and two in the mornings, period 1. I don't know if they're half asleep or if they're keen to learn [but they are very quiet and passive].

This teacher seems to be saying that what he counts as 'working well' is quietly accepting the material. The context of the lesson is obviously import-ant; first thing in the morning. He suggests that it is easier to carry out his goals under these circumstances.

The following quote by a St James teacher suggested that 'working well' in this school went further than pupils accepting quietly the material presented by the teacher:

> The one theme that goes through it all [my teaching] is that I want the children to be confident in the class with me, confident of being treated fairly, of being given an ear, of being allowed an atmosphere in which they can develop and they can work.

Having set this framework for the pupils, the St James teacher then explains that she expects pupils to recognise the value of work and to apply themselves to the material. A more active response is expected from the class:

> . . . I'm watching round the room to an extent, I'm not allowing the class to sit and doze . . . I'm not satisfied unless I have a good response from them. I try to involve as many people as I can, so that they've got to be on their toes all the time.

What we have suggested so far is that how teachers view their teaching will have important effects on which goals they select for pupils and how they go about achieving these goals. We have already said that we are making no prior judgements on this but rather that teachers need to examine their own views of what teaching is all about. Of course, as in any solution, there will be benefits and costs.

Conclusion

In this chapter we have examined how our four schools varied in their views of the purposes of teaching. These views, in turn, affected what teachers counted as working well in their classrooms. We have also pointed out that these views were affected by a number of important conditions, perhaps the most significant being the school's view of the pupil. Both the view of the pupil and the view of teaching were influenced by other pressures such as the school's catchment area and its past history. Each school, then, had a particular culture into which new staff and pupils were socialised.

It is important to remind ourselves that we are not referring to 'effective teaching', but rather to how the school's view of teaching affects discipline in the classroom. We have looked at a small, though integral, part of the teaching process, classroom discipline. Certainly, teachers were not asked to talk about their discipline as an isolated factor in classroom life. From the outset of the research we adopted a broad view of discipline, described earlier as 'creating an atmosphere which allows learning to take place'. The researcher's prompt in the classroom teachers' interviews, 'What did you do to make the class work well?', deliberately continued with this broad conception.

An earlier review of the literature (Johnstone and Munn, 1987) alerted us to the contextual nature of school and classroom discipline. The analysis of our data has reinforced the significance of this context. Just as there is no recipe knowledge for effective teaching there is, similarly, no recipe knowledge for implementing and maintaining effective discipline in classrooms. This may come as disappointing news to students, beginning teachers and those responsible for managing and advising in schools. There are a number of different ways of working well in classrooms, and these are explored in Chapters 6 and 7.

Table 3.1: Benefits and costs: The teachers' view of teaching influences classroom discipline

Teaching as a progression through a set body of knowledge	Teaching as the motivation of pupils to learn	Teaching as containment of pupils unwilling to learn

HOW DOES THIS AFFECT WHICH CLASSROOM RULES APPLY?

Rules are set in advance so that everyone can progress through the work.	Rules are negotiable and they have to be capable of a rational explanation.	Rules are prescriptive and restrictive.

Benefits
- Pupils are clear about what classroom rules are.
- Classroom rules encourage work related behaviour.

Benefits
- Rules will be changed if they seem inappropriate.
- It is more likely that pupils and teachers agree on the value of the rules.

Benefits
- The teacher is seen to be in charge.
- Pupils know how far they can go.

Costs
- There is little room for negotiation of the rules.

Costs
- Explaining the rationality of the rules takes time from subject teaching.
- There is a potential threat to the autonomy of the teacher.

Costs
- Pupils feel alienated by the rules.
- Rule enforcement becomes time-consuming.

HOW DOES THIS AFFECT SANCTIONS?

Sanctions have to be applied with minimal disturbance to the work of the class.	Sanctions have to be seen to be fair and rehabilitative.	Sanctions have to be seen to be punitive.

Benefits
- The majority of pupils are able to get on with their work.

Benefits
- Most of the pupils accept the justice of sanctions.

Benefits
- Pupils are made aware of the penalties for indiscipline.

Costs
- Offences which do not disturb the work of the class are less likely to be punished.
- Pupils may fail to learn about the consequences of rule breaking if sanctions are less visible.

Costs
- Time and resources necessary to explain sanctions may take time from other areas of the curriculum.

Costs
- Pupils may be alienated from the school's values.
- Sanctions are seen by pupils as only punitive. Their rehabilitative value is not recognised.

HOW DOES THIS AFFECT REWARDS?

Rewards are tied to effort in making progress through this set body of knowledge.	Rewards are tied to both work and behaviour.	Rewards are for passive, quiet behaviour.

Benefits
- Work progress is seen as highly valued.

Benefits
- Rewards are available to a wide range of children.

Benefits
- A starting position for work is set up.

Costs
- Less able pupils are unlikely to be rewarded.

Costs
- The value of work is less central.

Costs
- Quiet behaviour is as important as learning.

HOW DOES THIS AFFECT PASTORAL CARE?

Guidance is seen as helping teachers by dealing with those pupils unable or unwilling to cope with the work pattern.

Guidance is seen as helping teachers by encouraging personal and social development in all pupils.

Guidance is seen as helping teachers by dealing with pupils unable or unwilling to cope with teacher expectation of passive behaviour.

Benefits
- The value of work is emphasised.

Benefits
- The value of personal and social maturity is emphasised.

Benefits
- Guidance provides support for the teacher.

Costs
- The development of personal and social skills is seen as less important by teachers and pupils.
- Guidance may find it difficult to pursue a social education programme.

Costs
- Some subject teaching time will be sacrificed for time spent on personal and social development.

Costs
- The development of personal and social skills is seen as less important by teachers and pupils.

Exploring your school's view of teaching

Finding out whether there is a school-wide view of teaching within your school is no easy matter. We recognise the difficulty for a member of any social organisation in 'making the familiar strange'. The following questions, however, might help teachers to get started. How you do this is a matter of personal choice. You could begin, for example, by talking informally to colleagues and pupils about what the rules, sanctions and rewards mean.

- Begin by thinking carefully about whether there is a dominant purpose of teaching in your school. Then talk to colleagues to get their views. Do they have similar ideas or concerns?
- Examine the school rules. Where are they to be found? Within the school brochure? In corridors? How did these school rules gain prominence? Why? How are they communicated? Are they fixed/flexible? Does this tell you anything about the school's view of teaching?
- Look at the rules in your classroom, asking similar questions. Are your rules the same as the school rules? How are the rules communicated to the pupils? Are parents aware of classroom rules? What do pupils think about the rules? How can you find out? Ask a group to discuss the rules or to write about them for the school magazine or brochure.
- Consider the sanctions that are available in the school. What messages do these sanctions convey? Discuss school-wide sanctions with your

colleagues. Are you using these sanctions in similar ways? Ask a group of pupils to write about sanctions.
- Think about which rewards and incentives are offered in your school. Are they offered for a particular type of behaviour? What does this tell you about the goals in your school? Are all staff rewarding the same type of behaviour? Is there a school-wide reward system? Should there be?

References

Hammersley, M. (1975) *A Staff-room Ideology*, mimeographed paper.

Hargreaves, D. H. (1978) What teaching does to teachers, *New Society*, 9 March.

Hargreaves, D. H. (1980) The occupational culture of teachers, in P. Woods, (ed.) *Teacher Strategies: Explorations in the Sociology of the Secondary School*, Croom Helm, London.

Johnstone, M. and Munn, P. (1987) *Discipline in School: A Review of 'Causes' and 'Cures'*, Scottish Council for Research in Education, Edinburgh.

Lacey, C. (1970) *Hightown Grammar: The School as a Social System*, University Press, Manchester.

Woods, P. (1979) *The Divided School*, Routledge & Kegan Paul, London.

Woods, P. (1980) *Pupil Strategies*, Croom Helm, London.

4
MANAGEMENT MAKES A DIFFERENCE

What do we mean by management? The senior management team or board of studies in a secondary school are the people who make the policies and who see that these policies are implemented. Typically, a board of studies consists of the headteacher, a deputy head and two or more assistant headteachers. The number of senior management posts below that of headteacher varies according to the number of pupils in the school. Each member of the board of studies is allocated both general and specific duties within the school by the headteacher. Specific duties would be responsibility for the guidance system, for example, or for the curriculum. General duties are a matter of agreement between the headteacher and senior management, and would include duties relevant to good discipline, for example supervision of key public areas of the school such as the entrance hall or dining hall.

The next level of management is the head of department, who has a key role in implementing the policies. The head of department is responsible for the day-to-day running of the subject department and for what is taught there. Of course, as a subject specialist, the head of department may look to sources outside the school, to professional bodies or national guidelines for definitions of his or her task. The autonomy of the head of department is an important point to which we return in Chapter 5. In this chapter, we are concerned with the head of department in relation to senior management and to overall discipline in the school.

The pastoral care team in Scottish schools is a group drawn from different departments. The team is headed by an assistant headteacher and includes principal teachers of guidance (the post of principal teacher being equivalent to that of head of department) and assistant principal teachers of guidance The role of the principal teacher (guidance) is defined by the way in which the headteacher organises the whole guidance system. Nevectheless, the principal teacher (guidance) will have a large case-load of pupils to advise and a great deal of paperwork to manage. He or she will also have responsibilities as a teacher within a subject department. Again, there are implications for the autonomy of the principal teacher (guidance) in that his or her role is defined by the headteacher, and that he or she also has subject teaching responsibilities. We will return to this in Chapter 5, but here we will look at how the headteacher and the senior management team see the role of guidance staff or pastoral care in relation to good discipline in the school.

As a key idea, the simple statement that the senior management team makes a difference to how discipline works in a school seems obvious. Teachers would say that of course good management helps, bad management hinders. However, the management team operates in a particular context, a real school with pupils and teachers and day-to-day problems. What is good management in one context may be not so good in another. We do not intend to pursue some sort of definitive description of good management, but to focus on the key idea that how the management team goes about its task carries messages about what is important in the school. The ways in which management says and does things affect what counts as good discipline, both intentionally and unintentionally.

The broad aims of all schools are likely to be similar, focusing on successful learning and reasonable pupil behaviour. Of course, the definitions of successful learning and reasonable behaviour stem from the individual school's view of the pupil, as we argue in Chapter 2. Senior management's policies designed to achieve these aims may be rather different, and in themselves carry messages about discipline. This chapter looks at some ways in which management operates, how messages are given and what these messages are. We hope that this will help teachers to focus on management in their own schools, and to go beyond the simple 'good' or 'not so good' to ask what is it that characterises management. What message does management in your school give? What are the implications for good discipline? For example, in each of the case-study schools, members of the board of studies were allocated responsibility for a specific year group or groups of pupils. This person was then the one to whom heads of department turned, if a child in that year group became a more serious discipline problem. The senior management team in each school had to decide how these year-head posts would be allocated, to make best use of the skills of the team. This could have implications for discipline in the school. In Braidburn, the person allocated fourth-year pupils was seen by pupils and teachers as one of the strictest teachers in the school. The intentional message was that management were prepared to deal strictly with indiscipline. The unintentional message was that fourth year pupils were most likely to be troublesome.

We present some examples of how senior staff in different schools went about the job of managing, and contrast different approaches. We also look at what the specific approach implied for the school in terms of benefits and costs. The main body of the chapter looks at how management operates in relation to three main areas of importance to discipline in a school:

- dealing with indiscipline;
- promoting good discipline;
- the role of the pastoral care system.

The concluding section of the chapter examines possible explanations behind these different ways of managing.

Dealing with indiscipline

How senior staff dealt with indiscipline was to many teachers the most visible way in which the board of studies and headteacher made a difference in their school. Across the four schools, definitions of indiscipline were similar, ranging from talking out of turn in class to an outright confrontation between pupil and teacher. What differed from school to school was staff perception of the prevalence of indiscipline, and staff decisions about what could be dealt with in class and what passed on up the line for more weighty sanctions. These differences, we suggest, arose as much from different ways of managing as from genuine differences in pupil behaviour.

In Easthill alone, there was an additional managerial responsibility relevant to indiscipline. This was the Pupil Support Unit (PSU). The unit had a dual role in the school, one which was very difficult to sustain. At one level, the unit gave teachers support by taking in briefly any pupil locked in confrontation with a teacher. This allowed time out or cooling off for both parties. However, beyond this purely supervisory function, the unit worked with some difficult or disaffected pupils in the hope of reintegrating them into the mainstream school. These two roles were potentially opposed; the first supported teachers, or was seen to do so, while the second supported pupils already defined as 'trouble'. This dual role may have been more difficult in a linear system such as Easthill's than in a more flexible collegiate system where professional contact between colleagues was encouraged. In Easthill, both mainstream staff and unit staff related in a linear way to management, which then had to interpret and mediate between the two. This placed great demands on management, in terms of skills and sensitivity.

In all the schools, senior staff were brought into formal contact with problems of discipline through the referral chain. This was a mechanism described in greater or lesser detail for the staff in the school handbooks. Basically, the referral chain set out step by step each stage in dealing with a problem which the teacher considered had to be passed on and could not be dealt with in the classroom. The teacher would refer the problem pupil to the head of department as the first stage. If the head of department felt further action was needed, he or she would refer the problem pupil to the year head, a member of the board of studies. If he or she, in turn, felt further action was needed, the headteacher would be involved. At each of these stages the sanctions available were similar, that is lines, written exercises, appropriate punishment tasks, and 'telling off'. The difference was that the sanctions were being applied by progressively more senior members of staff, thereby conveying to pupils the increasing seriousness of the offence. Suspension from school and exclusion from school were sanctions which only the headteacher could apply.

The key to the successful operation of this referral chain was the setting up of some form of filter, so that serious offences were separated from less serious but highly annoying offences. Serious sanctions could then be applied sparingly, and the involvement of senior staff held its value as a grave step. Senior staff in each school encouraged a filtering out of problems so that only serious ones reached them. How they did this differed from school to school and had different benefits and costs, as we intend to show by contrasting two of our schools.

In Braidburn, management placed great emphasis on consensus, on a collegiate approach. The headteacher felt that this was vital: 'We needed a total team . . . you try to get folk around who are of similar mind'. Senior staff encouraged consensus by talking to staff, and by encouraging staff to talk to one another across departments. They were to be found occasionally in the staff-room at breaks and frequently took part in conversation about incidents in the daily life of the school, including any indiscipline. These conversations ranged from informal feedback to staff who had passed a pupil on to them to be dealt with, to jokes and anecdotes about pupils' behaviour. The feeling of camaraderie was encouraged by the fact that the members of the board of studies (although not the headteacher) were genuine members of subject departments themselves; each had quite a heavy teaching load. They did a lot of talking to teachers informally on the way to lessons and in subject work rooms as well as in the staff-room. Teachers did a lot of talking to other teachers, to their head of department and to other heads of department. Official policy emphasised loose boundaries between departments, and stressed ideas such as faculties and cross-subject courses. As one teacher said: 'The staff is a close staff. In other schools people tend to take themselves off to various hiding places, whereas everybody comes into the staff-room here, with a few exceptions . . . I think there's a lot more to-ing and fro-ing about children, you discuss, you're more aware'.

It seemed to us that, in Braidburn, senior management had created a first filter at teacher level, through the way in which they managed. Their approach was to encourage teachers to agree on what counted as good discipline and indiscipline. Staff regarded the same kinds of pupil misbehaviour as ʲrritating, and were agreed on the kinds of pupil misbehaviour which had to be passed on. For example, it was formally suggested in the staff handbook that 'extending and shortening the referral chain can have advantages in different circumstances'.

It seems likely that management reliance on teachers to use the referral chain sensibly could only be possible if teachers did agree on the kinds of offence to pass on either speedily or step by step.

The benefit of this consensual filtering was that the more weighty sanctions were reserved for serious offences. Teachers took responsibility for their classes, and management were not overloaded. There was another benefit arising from senior management's push for consensus. In Braidburn, most teachers took responsibility for discipline in the public areas of the school: the corridors and stairs, for example. This attitude was helped by the readiness of management to intervene. In fact, it had been known for the referral chain to be short-circuited from the top down, for the head to deal with a minor offence if he witnessed it, cutting out the head of department who might have been expected to deal with it. This was somewhat wryly noted by other senior staff: 'One of the things the head is guilty of – if I can put it like that – is that he tends to step in . . . He tends to break his own guidelines'.

The cost of this way of managing was that the informal approach could lead to misunderstanding. If teacher views were collected individually or in the passing, then open acknowledgement of staff input to decision making might not be made. This could lead to a feeling of not really being consulted professionally. One teacher new to the school, although recognising informal contact with management, felt that 'it's very dictatorial, there really are very few committees here, we're not involved in decision-making'.

The informal, consensual approach in Braidburn was a managerial decision. It may also reflect the dominant view of the child in Braidburn as an important part of the community of that particular town and of the school (see Chapter 2). This view meant that staff had to be flexible enough to accept the children as they were, while demanding that pupils met the school standards of work and of behaviour. The balance between accepting pupils and changing pupils was a delicate one which a formal, linear system might not be able to sustain. An informal, consensual system allowed for negotiation and change without confrontation, thus preserving the school community.

In Oldtown, where there was a more formal, linear approach to management, a referral chain was also in operation. Once again, the board of studies had to filter serious from trivial offences in order to maintain the impact of senior staff involvement. There were two main ways in which senior staff accomplished this. First, the headteacher set out a very clear written policy on what the standard teacher response to various kinds of indiscipline should be. This policy was derived from consultation with staff via a formal *ad hoc* committee of teachers and senior staff. The committee collected examples of successful policies to deal with classroom indiscipline from teachers throughout the school, and codified this. The staff handbook also contained clear and useful guidelines on classroom management, on ways of preventing indiscipline. The benefit of this approach was that all teachers could see in black and white what the expected pattern of response was. It will be remembered that Braidburn relied on a more informal approach to achieving an expected pattern.

The second strand to senior management's approach in Oldtown was a reliance on the head of department as a 'middle manager'. Oldtown gave considerable autonomy to heads of department to manage their subject departments in ways that seemed appropriate to them. The heads of department had to convince the teachers in the subject departments to accept the standardisation of responses to indiscipline and to filter out serious from trivial offences. However, they differed in their view of how standardised such responses should be:

> Every teacher has for every class they teach a register – it's a record of the teacher's work, and also a disciplinary log too . . . The teachers have confidence in it. Everyone in the department adheres to it. Within the department it's very effective.

> Within the department there are different styles; it all comes down to personality. Some are quite strict and consistent, others have more of a friendly approach and do seem to get the results anyway.

The important point was that senior management were screened out of dealing with minor offences. The head of department appeared to exercise a degree of choice over a stricter or looser adherence to the standardisation of responses to indiscipline.

The benefit of this system was the reliance on the heads of department, thereby enhancing their middle management role. The senior management team had to devote its energies mainly to convincing the heads of department of the wisdom of their policies, and the end result was the same as that in Braidburn. Senior staff in both schools did not feel that they were overloaded with discipline problems which could have been dealt with effectively lower down the referral chain. The cost of this linear way of managing was that departments could disagree about dealing with indiscipline. A second cost was that areas of the school outside the department could be seen as somebody else's business; as one teacher pointed out: 'I have seen teachers walking past incidents which I wouldn't walk past'.

In Oldtown, management appeared to have created a first filter at head of department level, through the way in which they managed. Management used formal, paper policies and relied upon the heads of department to expand and flesh out these policies. Teachers felt that on the whole they were happy with how indiscipline was dealt with in their department, whether they agreed on a standard response to indiscipline, or agreed to disagree. Teachers felt that other staff in the school, perhaps even whole departments, were different in how they dealt with indiscipline. Some degree of difference across departments was seen as acceptable. In Oldtown, subject specialism was important. This in itself 'justified' different ways of dealing with indiscipline.

Dealing with serious offences

When indiscipline was defined as serious enough to pass right on to the end of the referral chain, the pupil in question was usually sent 'to the office'. In other words, senior management dealt with the problem. There were contrasts among the schools in the way 'the office' responded. In Braidburn, senior staff made their punishment of that pupil visible, if punishment in the form of a written exercise rather than a task such as litter collection was deemed appropriate. The pupil sat at an entry to the school, near stairs which were used by many classes. The benefit of this was that other pupils and teachers saw that senior staff were dealing with indiscipline. In Oldtown, senior staff kept the pupil in the administration block, literally screened from public view. Even staff or the occasional pupil who entered 'the office' might not be aware of the pupil being punished. The senior status of the person giving the punishment was important; being seen to be punished was not. The benefit of this was that publicity and perhaps sneaking admiration from other pupils was avoided.

In Braidburn, many people were aware of management involvement in dealing with indiscipline. In Oldtown, only those immediately affected were aware. In Braidburn, many people were made aware when there were behaviour problems in the school. In Oldtown, only those immediately affected were aware. This may reflect the view of the child in each school. In Braidburn, the emphasis on the child as part of a specific community made it important for indiscipline to be dealt with in public. In Oldtown, the emphasis on the child as scholar made it more important not to distract other pupils from the goal of work. This latter view had an additional cost for senior staff, whose intervention was invisible to the majority of teachers.

The foregoing example focused on different ways of managing once indiscipline was passed up the referral chain. However, a way of managing which in itself stressed being visible around the school implied that, in the everyday course of events, visibility would bring senior staff into sight of pupil indiscipline. Teachers who saw senior staff passing along the corridor, speaking to pupils, reproving pupils if the need arose, gained a positive impression. The visibility of management brought an enormous benefit. However, as teachers watched management, management could in turn see the teachers; as one Oldtown teacher noted: 'Senior staff should be more visible . . . If you know somebody's likely to go past you pull yourself up'. Visibility increased senior management's knowledge of the teachers as well as the pupils.

The examples of dealing with indiscipline given in this section are just that, examples. They are not recipes. We have tried to emphasise the benefits and costs of dealing with indiscipline in different ways. Basically, in the two schools we have focused on, what was done about indiscipline was fairly similar. The difference lay in how management went about the job. This affected how a consensus was reached on what counted as indiscipline, and how serious offences were filtered out from trivial ones. Whichever way of managing indiscipline was used in the school, benefits and costs accrued. No particular way of managing had only benefits, or only costs.

The role of the headteacher

We have talked of the board of studies or senior management as if this were a unit. The unique powers of the headteacher in applying sanctions such as suspension have been referred to, but not the possible role of the headteacher as leader. This is a concept which has been noted as important in the managing of a school. In fact, in relation to good discipline, the headteacher was seen as a positive force in one pair of schools. This was in terms of personality or visibility rather than of the more general concept of 'leadership':

> The personality of [the headteacher] had a lot to do with it [good discipline in the school], his open, friendly personality. It's a friendly set up, caring for the children – it does seem to be true here.
>
>   (Teacher, Braidburn)

> The headteacher is accessible not only to teachers but to pupils. It surprised me at first . . . It's got disadvantages, but the pluses outweigh that . . . [This] . . . prevents the kind of no-go attitudes that the corridor or the yard is 'not my responsibility'.
>
>   (AHT, St James)

The visibility and approachability of the headteacher in both St James and Braidburn were seen as important in drawing the school together, but it was only in Braidburn that the teachers talked about leadership: 'The headteacher drives the school'. 'Every headteacher should stamp his own ideas, because I think that without a leader you don't have much'.

As noted in Chapter 1, Braidburn at the time of the research was experiencing a change of headteacher. This seemed to be the reason behind the more frequent mention in Braidburn of the idea of leadership. It was also the case that Braidburn had once had a very bad reputation in terms of discipline, and that the retiring headteacher was seen by older staff as personally instrumental in turning the school round, building on its strengths, so that it enjoyed an excellent local reputation. As one long-serving member of staff said: 'Discipline has to start at the top, and the headteacher we've just lost decided from the very start that the school was going to be a well run school. So it came from the top'.

Undoubtedly, the more extrovert style of leadership practised by the headteachers in Braidburn and St James had its effect. According to teachers in the schools, this kind of lead promoted positive feelings in the pupils, a feeling of belonging to the school.

In these schools, when the pupils wrote about the rules, senior staff were mentioned by name. However, pupils were more likely to write about senior staff, the headteacher in particular, as enforcing the rules rather than promoting positive feelings. The headteacher was the ultimate sanction and his name was quoted (often in emphatic block capitals) as dealing with indiscipline. This in itself was approved of, and seen as essential in running the school. After all, as one pupil wrote, if you don't keep the school rules 'people will think the headmaster is soft'. The pupils seemed to expect that the headteacher personally made sure that rules were kept.

In our other two schools, Easthill and Oldtown, a different kind of leadership obtained. In Easthill there was an acting headteacher, and the school itself was seen by staff as under threat of closure. In these circumstances, 'leadership' may have seemed more a matter of simply keeping the school ticking over. In Oldtown, the headteacher had by choice adopted a more team-based concept of leadership. His personal view was that a professional, established senior management team would be more appropriate to the situation in Oldtown than an extrovert, charismatic leader. This may well have been so, given the context of the school, but leadership by committee did seem to leave the staff faintly dissatisfied. Teachers knew who was in charge, but felt that 'they should be seen, be more visible, to be seen to be enforcing their own rules'.

The headteacher encouraged the enforcement of rules by working closely with the senior management team and with heads of department. There were regular meetings between senior and middle management to discuss problems and ways of making progress, but this work was invisible to the rest of the staff. The danger was that a low profile could be interpreted as lack of interest.

On the whole, when the teachers in our four schools spoke about the role of the headteacher they did not talk in terms of leadership, but in more simple terms of visibility, accessibility or friendliness. Of course, being visible or friendly is no guarantee of effective management, but it did seem to be the case that lack of visibility was seen, unfairly or not, as lack of interest in how classroom teachers were dealing with discipline.

The measurement of indiscipline

One of the questions which interested us was: did the school keep any records of indiscipline, and were these records used as a measure of how discipline in the school stood? It was also possible that records measuring consistent problems could be used as a lever to bring pressure to bear on the local authority for help in terms of a better staffing ratio, for example. In fact, all four schools kept records but these were, in the main, individual records of difficult pupils. In addition, all four schools kept an attendance record. In Oldtown and in Braidburn, any collation of the pupil records was seen as a fairly pointless exercise, given the small numbers of pupils seen as difficult, and the contextual variations in offences seen as minor. In Easthill and St James, some collation was made of exclusions, and Easthill also collated truancy figures in order to make comparisons between year groups. In both these schools, the collation of figures had been used as tangible evidence to back up a request for more resources, with some degree of success. In St James, the exclusion figures were also posted in the staff-room, to keep staff up to date with the situation.

The collation of data on indiscipline seemed to be a labour undertaken only if a potential benefit might accrue. Senior management and staff in all four schools noted the value of individual pupil records as kept by the pastoral care team. However, the more general collation of records depended upon the conditions in the school. Easthill and St James, with their urban and deprived catchment areas, saw collated records as useful. Braidburn and Oldtown, with their more settled catchment areas, did not. Besides, as the headteacher of Oldtown pointed out, simple numeric collation could be of little value as an index of good behaviour in a school: 'I don't think you can total up the number of misdemeanours and divide them by the number of pupils. Pupils will behave differently in different situations'.

Promoting good discipline

How did senior staff in the different schools go about the promotion of good discipline? In all the schools, good discipline was similarly defined in official statements of school policy. Key elements were pupil behaviour conducive to learning, behaviour showing courtesy and respect to staff and fellow pupils, safe movement within the school, and acceptable standards of appearance. Leaving aside dress, which some teachers saw as a controversial issue, and safety, which most people saw as common sense, the broad and general ideals remained. Within each school, one or other of these ideals apparently had assumed more prominence, from what teachers said, for that particular school at that particular time. This is not to say other ideals were discarded; it was more a question of priorities. It also emerged that senior management and teachers were in broad agreement about the priority in their school, what they would like to promote as good discipline. The real question was, how did management go about this? Did the way in which they promoted good discipline make a difference?

In this section we contrast the ways in which management in two different schools promoted good discipline. The schools are St James and Braidburn, which have been shown to be quite similar and which were also similar in the ways in which senior management worked, in that both operated a collegiate style of management. Our purpose is to emphasise the fact that differences in management are a matter of degree, and that even where management seems to work in similar ways the actual context of the school has its effect on policies.

In St James, the headteacher firmly believed that school could make a difference to pupil behaviour, that the school could promote good discipline even among pupils from disadvantaged backgrounds. This belief was promoted among the staff by encouraging discussion and negotiation over policies, as well as by tangible measures taken by senior staff. These measures seen as promoting good discipline were:

- regular assemblies of all the pupils;
- setting up the merit league to reward class discipline;
- contacting parents with good news and praise of pupils;
- learning the names of all the pupils, to let them know they belonged;
- being visible around the school, being seen to be interested in the pupils and in good discipline.

Underlying these measures was management's emphasis on the school as a community of people working rationally towards agreed objectives. However, these objectives were firmly defined by the school. As one subject teacher stated: 'Lower standards are not acceptable . . . There's a standard of work [of which] we keep a record'.

In the same way, the community was defined by the school through the denominational context. This context gave opportunities for the expression of group solidarity in religious festivals and assemblies; as a St James' teacher noted: 'Not all the teachers in the school are Catholics, but you find a lot of non-Catholics in the school take part in religious services'.

The benefits for those pupils who agreed to belong to the group, to conform with school expectations of good discipline were in terms of affirmation of worth. As one child said of the headteacher: 'He makes me feel like a person'.

However, the cost of setting up any group is that by default it also defines outsiders. For example, the merit card system whereby well-behaved classes were rewarded also ensured that some classes were unlikely to be rewarded.

The promotion of good discipline in St James seemed to reflect a particular emphasis by management on the school as a forward-looking community. Staff and pupils were aware of benefits in this; the costs were in terms of the work needed to integrate pupils who for one reason or another chose to reject the school community. This made the job of the pastoral care team in St James a vital one. They had to persuade alienated or deviant pupils to accept the school's standards of behaviour and of work.

In Braidburn, management took a similar approach to the promotion of good discipline, differing only in degrees of emphasis. However, this difference was an important one. Good discipline was seen as arising out of matching what the community wanted with what the school could give. Although the school set down standards of behaviour and of work, definitions of 'work' were negotiable. We do not mean to imply that pupils were given work only to keep them busy and occupied, or allowed to do what they liked. On the contrary, the flexibility of management and willingness to consider curricular change gave the message that the school could find the *right* work for all its pupils. This belief was promoted among staff through informal discussion and through the emphasis placed on consensus within the school in seeking to do the best for the pupils from this specific community. The measures taken in this school to promote good discipline were:

- learning the names of all pupils, to let them know they belonged;
- being visible around the school, being seen to be interested in the pupils and in good discipline;
- using a familiar Scots language register rather than formal English, to emphasise the common roots of teachers and pupils;
- experimenting with and changing the curriculum, to meet the needs of as many different pupils as possible;
- offering a wide variety of extra-curricular activities not available in the community.

Senior management in Braidburn were highly aware of the given nature of the local community. This was a context with which the school had to deal: a strong local community. The measures taken by management to promote good discipline were measures designed to emphasise that school and community could work together for the good of the children. The major way of promoting the pupils' interests was through the kind of courses offered and through a willingness to change to meet pupil needs.

Teachers in Braidburn spoke enthusiastically of Standard Grade and the changes brought about by this new system: 'The new syllabus has gone in, the kids have something to work towards. The discipline problem that was in that group, the bottom ability group, it's just disappeared. It's unbelievable . . . It's the best thing that's happened to us, Standard Grade.'

Other teachers spoke equally enthusiastically of pupils and the traditional exam system: 'It's our high flyers, our good kids. We have to say to our kids that you don't have to be born within a certain social structure, with any of the wonderful things their parents believe they need to go on to [higher education].

What these teachers had in common was their view of the curriculum as providing an incentive to pupil work, and thus an incentive to good discipline. Of course, this is not unique. Many schools are offering a range of courses to their pupils. Many teachers would agree that an appropriate curriculum promotes good discipline. However, in Braidburn the willingness of the staff to consider change, to consider alternatives and if necessary create courses to suit their pupils reflected senior management's views. The promotion of good discipline in Braidburn seemed to follow the emphasis by senior staff on the school as serving a specific community with specific needs. The board of studies attempted to lessen the distance between teachers and pupils, and to offer attractive and interesting learning. Staff were very aware of the benefits to discipline arising from this, but there were costs in terms of professional commitment and effort. Materials had to be prepared, reading had to be done, courses had to be designed and redesigned to meet pupils' needs. Not all teachers might be willing to shoulder these costs.

As stated earlier, we cannot offer recipes for the promotion of good discipline. We have given some examples from two of our schools illustrating the steps taken to promote good discipline. In each, these steps reflect the history and context of the school, as well as the different messages given by rather similar styles of management.

Good discipline and rewards

One way of promoting good discipline is to reward the behaviour valued by the school. In all of our schools, teachers and pupils seemed less conscious of rules for good behaviour than of penalties for bad behaviour. Nevertheless, each school had ways of approving the pupil behaviour seen as good discipline. In Oldtown, the formal reward system gave approval to 'academic and sporting success'. Senior pupils were also rewarded or given formal approval by their selection as prefects by the staff. These rewards, and their control by management, emphasised the values of the school. The cost was that some pupils, who could not aspire to these rewards, may have turned against a system which excluded them from the start. The linear system in Oldtown allowed freedom to heads of department (see Chapter 5), and within departments some teachers, too, could have freedom to give rewards. If such rewards were given by individuals or departments, they did not come to our attention. The formal reward system, which encapsulated the school values, was the more prominent.

In Easthill, which also had a linear system of management, the deficit view of the pupil undercut such a reward structure. Furthermore, the strong role of middle management in the linear system had introduced a contradictory element to rewards. The PSU at Easthill was a department which dealt with disruptive and disaffected pupils. To encourage these pupils to come to school and to work, the PSU staff gave little rewards and treats, and took these pupils on outings. Pupils and teachers in the main school sometimes saw this as a reward for bad behaviour. As one Easthill pupil wrote: 'I know some people who have been sent to [the PSU] a number of times, yet when any activity, to go anywhere or do anything in this school comes up, it is the people who are badly behaved that are chosen'.

This criticism may reflect an inevitable tension between the punitive and the therapeutic responses to pupil indiscipline, but it seems that in Easthill the *lack* of matching formal rewards may have exacerbated perceptions of the PSU as rewarding bad behaviour.

In the two collegial schools, some formal rewards were given; we have noted the merit league in St James, and its potential problems recognised by school management (see Chapter 2). However, the more informal, collegial management system seemed to rely on praise to acknowledge pupil achievement rather than formal rewards. Again, in St James, the headteacher wrote to all parents of first-year pupils, praising their children's behaviour. Of course, this can be seen as a shrewd political move to promote parental support, but it does indicate that, in St James, praise was seen as a mechanism of reward for appropriate behaviour. In Braidburn, the headteacher took a similar step in writing a formal letter of thanks to those staff who, during the school year, had made some extra contribution to the general good of the school. This, too, can be seen as a shrewd political move, but it also emphasises the use of praise in the school.

The benefit of praising a variety of pupil achievements, and using praise as a reward, seems to be that a good relationship is set up between pupils and teachers. In both St James and Braidburn, teachers and pupils felt that this was the case. The cost might be that academic status or success is seen by pupils as only one kind of achievement among several possibles. It may also be more difficult for staff to sustain such a personal and affective approach consistently and genuinely. To encourage staff in this may require a lot of managerial input.

Management, pastoral care and discipline

How senior staff saw the role of pastoral care had consequences for whole school discipline. The structure of pastoral care in Scottish secondary schools is not one of separate counsellors, as in the USA. Each Scottish guidance teacher or member of the pastoral care team is also a subject teacher. All pastoral care posts are promoted posts, either as assistant principal teacher or principal teacher of guidance. The number of guidance teachers in a school reflects the number of pupils, and in each school the overall head of this guidance department is usually a member of the board of studies, the assistant headteacher (guidance). The task of pastoral care staff is to advise and counsel all pupils and to deal with pupil welfare in any way that is appropriate. Each guidance teacher has a case-load of pupils, sometimes allocated on an alphabetical basis, otherwise on a horizontal year system.

Guidance teachers are in an anomalous position. They have subject-specific responsibilities, yet their role is to be of help to all staff, to counsel and advise all pupils. To achieve some part of the aims of pastoral care, guidance staff must have some kind of entry into other teachers' areas of responsibility. Their own dual role as guidance teachers and subject teachers can help with this. It can also help that pastoral care alone of all the school departments may have as its head of department a member of the board of studies. Other members of the board of studies may also be members of subject departments, but rarely heads of subject departments. Senior management has immediate access to the concerns of pastoral care and can define how the pastoral care is carried out. We illustrate some ways in which the definition of the pastoral care role has had a specific effect on good discipline.

In all the schools, the pastoral care team was formally allocated a counselling role, to help pupils with problems great or small. It was recognised by all staff that these problems would for some pupils inevitably be related to behaviour or work habits. However, the non-punitive nature of pastoral care was stressed by all of the management teams, in accord with the views expressed in *More than Feelings of Concern* (CCC, 1986). In Easthill, where the situation was an extreme one of crisis management, this was expressed succinctly by a member of senior staff; guidance was 'more like the Red Cross than the army'.

While agreeing that pupils were not sent to them to be punished, the pastoral care team in all the schools said that they would tell a pupil clearly if they thought his or her behaviour had been wrong. In fact, pastoral care staff in all four schools spoke in rather similar ways and had similar conceptions of their task. However, pastoral care operated rather differently in each of the schools. The way in which senior management defined the role of pastoral care contributed to these differences.

In all of the schools, the pastoral care team had two ways in which to influence good discipline. One way was through their work with those pupils who seemed to be alienated from the school. Pastoral care staff had the task of reconciling these pupils into the life of the school. A second way was through work with all pupils; this usually took the form of a programme of social education. The idea behind this programme was, in general, the personal and social development of the pupil.

In Braidburn, the form teacher or register teacher was spoken of by management as 'front-line guidance'. In fact, *all* teachers in Braidburn were form teachers; the younger classes had two form teachers, one male and one female, the older classes had one form teacher. If form teachers were the first stage of pastoral care, then every teacher was involved in pastoral care. However, the form teachers were not involved in the school's social education programme. This was devised and taught by those teachers in promoted guidance posts. Senior management had established a clear status for pastoral care as in the service of harmony in the school; an important element of this was their teaching role in the social education programme. The teaching aspect of pastoral care was clearly set out in the staff handbook. Communication between subject teachers and pastoral care staff was encouraged, to avoid the danger of overlap in the curriculum between a subject area and what could be part of social education. Communication between all subject teachers and guidance was encouraged through the way in which the form teacher system operated. The promotion of good discipline through integrating the pupil into society was the responsibility of the pastoral care team, but subject teachers were made aware of this aspect of the role of pastoral care through the policies of senior management.

In Oldtown, the form teacher or register teacher was also spoken of by management as 'front-line guidance'. In fact, it was not really clear how form teachers became form teachers. As one subject teacher jokingly suggested: 'Be in the wrong place at the wrong time! . . . People are *asked*'.

There had been a social education programme in Oldtown, devised and taught by teachers in promoted guidance posts. This programme had been confined to year one pupils, and had been discontinued to be re-thought. It was not clear why the programme had been halted, but one reason suggested by a subject specialist was that the school timetable had been altered. The creation of hour-long periods had perhaps given rise to departmental protest about chunks of subject teaching time being allocated to social education. The pastoral team themselves saw a teaching element as an essential part of their job; as one person said: 'As guidance teachers we spend too much time sitting at a desk, and not enough with the pupils'.

The pastoral care department in Oldtown was working on an alternative plan to timetable space for personal and social development, something it saw as helping promote good discipline in the school. The policies of senior management in Oldtown helped the pastoral care team to attain status as a department, to devise a social education programme based on their expertise. This was a benefit to pastoral care and, it was hoped, to the future of good discipline in the school. However, the linear nature of management in the school implied that pastoral care was one out of many departments, each valued by senior management for its specialist skills. The form teacher, the 'front-line guidance' person who was a full time subject specialist, might have been used to act as 'salesman' for the benefits to the school in sacrificing some subject teaching time for social education. The ways in which form teachers were selected did not seem to be directed at this outcome.

A second example of senior staff's view of the role of pastoral care staff comes from the different ways the schools used the behaviour card or supervision timetable with pupils who were in some sort of trouble or in some way alienated from the school. The behaviour card (see Chapter 2) was a daily record of the pupil's behaviour and effort, completed by each teacher the pupil saw during the day. In three of the schools, the idea of a behaviour card or supervision timetable was advocated by pastoral care staff as a means of rehabilitating problem pupils. This was seen as a crutch for weak pupils who might be drawn into further bad behaviour without it, or as a diagnostic tool forming the basis of discussion sessions between pupil and counsellor. In all the schools, pastoral care staff wanted to use those timetables sparingly, with pupils who might be responsive. In Oldtown, the managerial approach was to encourage staff towards standardisation in dealing with indiscipline. The managerial approach was also to work towards this through the establishment of clear guidelines for staff, to be passed on to teachers by the subject principal. The behaviour timetable as used by pastoral care was seen to be working in Oldtown. Pastoral care was also seen by teachers as a distinct department of the school. Almost inevitably, variants on the behaviour timetable materialised across subject departments, devaluing the strength of the original and causing problems for the very pupils the timetable was intended to help. As a member of the pastoral care team noted: 'What you are saying to the child is not only do you have to modify your behaviour, you [the pupil] have to deal with the school timetable and deal with these departmental behaviour timetables at the same time. They're just not capable of doing this'.

This unanticipated result of the management approach was a cost of that particular way of managing. Nevertheless, those teachers in departments which had taken up the behaviour timetable felt that it had helped them departmentally and that they had benefited.

We would repeat that senior management in the two schools contrasted were not idiosyncratic. In each case, the way they proposed to manage reflected the past history of the school, how the pupil was defined in that school, and what was seen as success for that school. In the more linear Oldtown, the costs of a school-wide pastoral care programme might turn out to be very high, in terms of departmental irritation and distraction from subject work, especially if social education were perceived by staff as irrelevant to most pupils. In the consensual Braidburn, the costs of such a programme might turn out to be equally high, in terms of demand upon the guidance team. The problem for the pastoral care team in trying to reconcile disaffected pupils to the school is also a problem of autonomy. However, in each school, the way in which management carried out its task had implications for pastoral care in relation to whole school discipline.

Conclusion

This chapter has addressed the idea that management makes a difference to school discipline policy and practice. Some examples of the differences that seemed to emerge from varying approaches have been given. At this point we should re-emphasise that these different approaches could and did seem quite correct or acceptable to many, even most, of the staff in any given school. The exception to this was in Easthill, the school with many problems. Here, senior management had a neutral, 'caretaker' role with no permanent headteacher in post. No personal criticism of the people in post was made, but there was unhappiness expressed by teachers about lack of direction. Although management had set up quite an elaborate system of committees and meetings to allow teachers to take an initiative in the area of discipline, teachers expected management to manage. In this school, individual teacher autonomy by default was not welcomed.

The reasons for the acceptability of management approaches seemed to lie in a complex mixture of how the pupils were defined, how teachers saw teaching, the catchment area and history of the school, and of course the real people involved. The stability of the catchment area seemed particularly important in that senior staff built up a knowledge of what to expect, and what would or would not be acceptable as a way of managing, given the sort of community the school served. It was also important to have a stable staff. This did not necessarily imply teachers staying on in the school. Stability could be achieved by the recruitment of like-minded people, teachers who would fit in. The criteria for selection of staff could be personal as much as professional.

It seemed that for teachers to understand the subtle signals sent out by the board of studies, they had to know what the school was about. In order to respond positively to how management operated, they had to *agree* with what the school was about. In three of our four schools, this was very clear. In Easthill, the fourth school, it was not.

To attempt to unravel this network fully, a more in-depth study of each school would be needed. This was not our aim, although we acknowledge the importance of uncovering the interconnections between the ingredients of the complex mixture that make up a school. Our aim was to explain, if we could, what happens in a range of schools, in terms of general but, we hope, convincing ideas.

There are constraints imposed upon management by the education authorities. We have noted in passing some specific historical or contextual constraints upon individual schools. Even within these constraints it appeared that the different schools were managed in distinctive ways. One pair of schools had what could be termed a more contractual approach, a hierarchical line management system. The other pair of schools had a more consensual approach, a collegiate management.

It seems that these two different styles represent a polarity of choice open to schools, although no real school could be wholly linear or wholly collegiate.

Each style crystallises a set of assumptions about schools and how they work. The major assumption behind both extremes is that pupils, staff and management all value the same objectives. Where they differ is that in a linear structure management tends to agree that setting up a clear, precise system can take into account the day-to-day reality of school life. Most situations can be anticipated and catered for through clear rules of procedure. In a more flexible collegial system management tends to agree that open discussion, negotiation and renegotiation of rules, sanctions and rewards is the way to achieve common standards. Formal structures are less important than responding appropriately to discipline problems as they present themselves.

Table 4.1: Benefits and costs: Management makes a difference

Management through a formal linear system	Management through an informal collegiate system
HOW DID THIS AFFECT THE APPLICATION OF RULES?	
Management sought common standards of discipline through formal guidelines and empowered principal teachers to oversee common standards in their department.	Management sought common standards of discipline through informal persuasion and by encouraging open discussion of discipline amongst all staff.
Benefits	*Benefits*
• Expectations were clearly set out for all staff. • A subject department refined the application of rules to suit their subject.	• Rules themselves were negotiated or changed if teacher consensus required this. • Consensus encouraged application of the rules outside classrooms as well as inside.
Costs	*Costs*
• The way(s) rules were applied varied between department. • Teachers were less concerned with applying rules outside their own department.	• Informal persuasion left some staff feeling that they had not been consulted. • The push towards consensus made some staff feel inadequate if their views about the rules differed from the majority.
HOW DID THIS AFFECT THE APPLICATION OF SANCTIONS?	
Management suggested a hierarchy of sanctions. Management were involved with application of sanction only when the offence was seen as serious.	Management suggested a hierarchy of sanctions and acknowledged that this might sometimes be changed by circumstances. Management could be involved with the application of sanctions for more minor offences.
Benefits	*Benefits*
• If management did apply sanctions, both offence and punishment would be seen as serious. • Management did not become overloaded. • Teachers were encouraged to take responsibility for using sanctions in their own classroom. • Heads of Department had a clear middle management role. • Pupils remained in awe of senior staff.	• Management were seen by staff to be interested and helpful in dealing with indiscipline. • Management were seen by pupils as involved in the rules. • Teachers were encouraged to use their professional judgement in passing on problems. • Pupils were aware that all staff were involved in the use of sanctions.
Costs	*Costs*
• Teachers felt that senior staff were too distant and inaccessible.	• Management time spent on discipline meant less time for other tasks.

HOW DID THIS AFFECT REWARDS?

Management emphasised formal rewards as part of the system. Rewards were defined as such by management and praise was given to good work.

Management tried to give both formal and informal rewards. Rewards were of different types and at different levels and praise was given to different achievements.

Benefits
- The value system of the school was affirmed.
- This fostered a notion of high expectations – that standards were valued.
- A certain kind of behaviour was expected.

Benefits
- Different forms of pupil success might be rewarded.
- Rewards were seen by the pupil as attainable by most of the pupils.

Costs
- Rewards were unattainable for a number of pupils.
- Only a specific kind of pupil success was rewarded.

Costs
- There was some inconsistency in the use of rewards.
- Work was not the main focus of rewards.

HOW IS THE PASTORAL CARE SYSTEM AFFECTED?

Management stressed the importance of pastoral care as an autonomous department with subject status in the school. Contact with subject departments tended to be formal, written contact.

Management stressed the importance of pastoral care as an integral part of the school, working with and supporting subject staff. Contact with subject staff tended to be informal, verbal contact.

Benefits
- The professional expertise of pastoral care staff was recognised.
- Formal written contact meant that good records on pupils could be kept.

Benefits
- Pastoral care staff were viewed by other staff as supportive and non-threatening.
- Liaison between pastoral care and other staff was made easier.

Costs
- Advice from pastoral care to subject staff could be viewed as interference.
- Servicing a system of formal, written records took time from pastoral contact with pupils.

Costs
- If was more difficult for pastoral care staff to keep accurate and complete records.

Researching the school's management of discipline

Your own school may tend to a linear management or to a collegiate management. Either system could be effective in dealing with discipline problems. How could it be made more effective? The ideas we suggest here are for the consideration of management, at whatever level, and those interested in how their school is managed.

(1) Think of an example where senior staff and teachers communicated successfully about discipline.
- What made this successful?
- Who was involved?
- Was anyone left out? Why?

(2) Compare this with an example when senior staff and teachers did not communicate about discipline.
   ● Who was involved?
   ● How was information exchanged?
   ● Why did communication break down?
What does an analysis of these examples suggest about making communication about discipline more effective within your school's system?

In a linear system, people can feel cut off. Is this true in your school? We suggest you check your ideas by carrying out the following tasks:

(For unpromoted staff)
Keep a note for two weeks of:
   ● how often you see senior management;
   ● what they were doing (just passing, talking to staff, supervising pupils, escorting visitors);
   ● any personal communication to you from senior management (verbal, written, informal, specific, general).

(For promoted staff)
Keep a note for two weeks of:
   ● how often you are out of your office/base/classroom, around the school;
   ● when you are around the school (during class time, at break or lunchtime);
   ● who you saw (teachers, pupils, promoted staff, ancillary staff);
   ● who you spoke to (teachers, pupils, promoted staff, ancillary staff);
   ● which parts of the school you visited (classrooms in one department, in several departments, staffroom, library, guidance room etc).

In a collegiate system, staff may take discipline standards for granted and agreement can lead to complacency.
   ● Ask probationer teachers or teachers new to the school to list the strong points about discipline in their departments. Are they comparable?
   ● Look back over the year at staff meetings. How many were there? Were staff participants or audience?
   ● Are there reviews of discipline? If so, who is involved – is it a broad range of staff?

References

Consultative Committee on the Curriculum (1986) *More than Feelings of Concern*, HMSO, Edinburgh.

Morgan, C. (1976) Management in education: dissimilar or congruent? *E321 Management in Education*, Open University Press, Milton Keynes.

Morgan, C., Hall, V. and MacKay, H. (1983) *A Handbook on Selecting Senior Staff for Schools*, Open University Press, Milton Keynes.

5
THE INFLUENCE OF DEPARTMENTAL AND TEACHER AUTONOMY ON DISCIPLINE

Autonomy is a complex idea which may be understood in various ways. We were less interested in the philosophical arguments than in the simpler notion about the freedom of subject departments and individual teachers to set their own standards of discipline. If a school is trying to improve discipline overall, the autonomy of teachers and departments is an important factor. This chapter tries to address two questions about autonomy. How much freedom can subject departments and individual teachers have to define what counts as good discipline in their departments and classrooms? If there are differences in degrees of freedom, do these differences have any implications for discipline policy and practice? The key idea we want to suggest is that: *the amount of autonomy given to subject departments and to individual teachers influences whole school discipline.*

We will discuss the operation of autonomy in our four schools, and how it affected discipline. Our evidence comes largely from school documentation and teacher interviews carried out across a range of subject departments in each school. The departments formally sampled in each of the four schools were: English; mathematics; art; physical education; science (including physics, chemistry and biology).

We chose teachers in these departments because our earlier pilot work had revealed that these were likely to be representative of different approaches to promoting and maintaining discipline. We asked our teachers to talk about whether there were common standards of discipline in their school and whether there were special definitions of discipline in subject departments, and about consistency among members of staff in dealing with indiscipline. We also gathered evidence from field notes taken in the schools. It was apparent from our data that our schools had rather different approaches to departmental autonomy and to the amount of freedom individual teachers had to define discipline. It is these different approaches and their influence on discipline which are the focus of this chapter.

Departmental autonomy

Let us begin by saying that all departments in the four schools operated within the broad framework of school rules and punishments outlined in the school brochures. However, the freedom of departments to extend and develop rules to suit their own particular circumstances differed quite sharply. Our four schools seemed to divide neatly into two pairs. One pair, Oldtown and Easthill, granted what we have called *extended departmental autonomy* to their subject departments. This means that the departments in these two schools had considerable freedom to 'run their own ship'. The teachers felt that colleagues outside their own departments had different definitions of good discipline and different ways of dealing with indiscipline. In Oldtown, for example, staff tended to agree that: 'If anything, maths is stricter'.

There were some teachers in these schools, too, who moved from their own department and departmental 'base' quite infrequently and who consequently felt unable to comment on the way other members of staff handled the question of discipline. As one Oldtown teacher said: 'I have no way of knowing what other teachers do because you know I am teaching and it's a claustrophobic occupation'.

In contrast, our other pair of schools, Braidburn and St James, granted what we have called *restricted departmental autonomy* to their subject departments. Staff in these schools talked about common approaches to discipline. Although there were a few references to special rules, such as safety in the science department, there was a general assumption that all subject departments had the same rules. Indeed one head of department in St James commented: 'Other members of staff are your best sources of help'.

In both schools, indiscipline was an accepted topic among teachers in general as well as within departments. Teachers in both schools would agree with the teacher in Braidburn who said:

> Anybody in the department and other members of staff meet in the staff common room and if you have a problem it's nice to hear that you're not the only one . . . That can be helpful, instead of letting the problem hang on you can find a way to get results.

Of course, some mention was made of differences between teachers in their approaches to discipline in both schools. However, where differences were cited, these were generally seen as purely personal or idiosyncratic, or reflections of different moods shown by the same person. Differences between staff because of their membership of a particular department were seldom mentioned.

How was discipline affected?

In Oldtown, extended departmental autonomy seemed a natural way of working in a school where scholastic achievement was highly valued. The departments were the locus of subject expertise and departmental staff had the professional skills to transmit that expertise to pupils. It then followed, as one head of department said, that 'discipline of course comes from the subject departments'.

It could be seen as entirely logical and consistent with the primacy given to departments as the purveyors of subject specialist knowledge and skills that they should also define what counted as good discipline while pupils were in the department. The benefit of extended autonomy in Oldtown was the explicit recognition of the importance and professionalism of the subject department. It assisted the departments to work towards the academic aims valued in Oldtown. It was for each department to set out their expectations of good behaviour which were designed to encourage pupils' achievement in the particular subject area.

The main cost of this extended autonomy was that it could lead to quite different standards in different departments. This was a cost of which senior management were well aware, and which they had been trying to counter through promoting a standard school policy on discipline. The focus on the department might also lead to another cost in terms of discipline outside the classroom. This point is discussed in Chapter 4, where it is suggested that, either through pressure of subject work or through a narrow contractual view of teaching, teachers might concern themselves with discipline only in the department. Again, this was a cost which managerial policy attempted to contain.

In Easthill, the extended autonomy for subject departments seemed to be a matter of default. The school was in a difficult situation; the referral system was overloaded as pupils continually broke rules. The actual composition of a given class could vary from week to week because of the high absenteeism rate. In addition, pupils were seen as uninterested in school work. In these circumstances, the autonomy of the department was not validated by the professional expertise of the teachers in transmitting their subject knowledge. What validated extended autonomy in this school was the support of colleagues and of the head of department in coping with the many problems. The department could even be seen as a place in which to hide from the potential confrontations in the public areas of the school; as one teacher admitted: 'I park the car at the back, beside the door to our department, and I keep out of the corridors if possible. Anything for a quiet life!'

The subject departments had become a vital source of help for the teachers, as had the Pupil Support Unit (PSU), which took in pupils for time out or cooling off. However, the extended autonomy given to subject departments included the unit, whose staff had the professional expertise and freedom to define their own role. The result was that subject departments and the PSU had different and opposing definitions of the role of the unit, as outlined in Chapter 4.

It is difficult to see any benefits from extended departmental autonomy in Easthill, other than in providing short-term relief for teachers. This could perhaps help them to cope with day-to-day difficulties in the classroom, but at a cost in terms of discipline in the whole school. Costs can be more readily seen than benefits in this difficult and unhappy situation. We do not wish to labour this point, but the school seemed caught in a spiral of depression which extended departmental autonomy did little to alleviate. In essence, extended departmental autonomy here was isolation. In Oldtown it represented professional independence in a fairly traditional framework.

In Braidburn and St James, the concept of a restricted autonomy did not reduce the importance of departments in dealing with indiscipline. However, the departments worked in similar ways, in step with the consensual viewpoint in the school. From time to time, and in rather different ways, individual departments made attempts to extend their autonomy. These attempts met with different degrees of success according to senior management's view of the risks posed to the collegiate framework in the school. Two examples from Braidburn illustrate this. The art department had its own special arrangements for offering advice to pupils contemplating a career in art, graphics, design and so on, bypassing the normal careers advice systems organised by guidance. Senior management permitted this on the grounds of the specialist knowledge of the art staff about career opportunities in the art field. In contrast, a new head of another department made an unsuccessful attempt to extend the department's autonomy by making special arrangements to stream pupils within the department and to prepare pupils for examinations on the basis of their performance on tests. Pupils who performed poorly on tests would not be prepared for particular public examinations. It was not unusual in Braidburn to have pupils set or streamed within subject departments. What was unusual was the lack of discussion of a number of alternatives for pupils, of flexible routes to entry for public examinations. What has this got to do with good discipline? In brief, this inflexibility was seen by other staff as a way of creating indiscipline. Other departments were seen as taking all pupils into account, as behaving in similarly flexible ways to encourage work from all ability levels. In the comparisons made by other staff and by management, the use that the head of department wanted to make of extended autonomy was viewed as out of step with the school. He was accordingly prevented from going ahead with this plan.

This example confirmed the idea that in the more consensual, collegiate kind of school, it was very difficult for a department to have extended autonomy. Autonomy could be extended, but only if the basis of increasing autonomy was seen as legitimate by senior management, as in the example of the department offering career guidance. Autonomy could not be increased if the likely result was seen by senior staff as counter to the successful working of the school.

The more linear management system allowed extended departmental autonomy within the overall discipline structure of the school. For any school management considering extended autonomy, one cost will be plain. What if departments start to deviate in how they deal with indiscipline? How can management ensure that good discipline is consistently promoted and yet allow heads of department the freedom which their professional status demands? Another cost might be a devaluing by teachers of the role of senior management. In terms of discipline maintenance, teachers could be more aware of their heads of department and less aware of senior managerial involvement unless it was given publicity. Much depends on the role that senior management sees itself as playing, as discussed in Chapter 4. This is a question to consider in analysing autonomy and management. Can potential costs be offset against the benefits of departmental autonomy? Extended autonomy may have benefits in encouraging cohesion within departments and this might be important in a large school where staff might feel anonymous. It could also enhance the professionalism of, in particular, principal teachers by recognising that their role extended beyond the management of the subject specific aspects of the work of the department to setting and maintaining standards of discipline appropriate to the department.

Restricted autonomy may seem more likely to have benefits in terms of a concerted all-school effort to keep good discipline, but here too there are costs to consider. Will heads of department accept their restricted autonomy? In our case-study schools, restricted autonomy was seen by most heads of department as an agreed consensus deriving from how their school worked. Not everyone accepted this. We referred to one attempt in Braidburn to achieve extended autonomy. If there were more such attempts, management would have serious problems. This is something to be considered, if restricted autonomy is seen as important to overall discipline; how can heads of department be persuaded to agree?

We should add that, in both extended and restricted autonomy, management will have inherited a historical situation, one derived from the context of the school and seen as suitable for that school. However, school discipline is not static. Pupils change, classes change and schools change. If change is to be positive and discipline to improve or remain good, the autonomy of departments must be considered.

The autonomous professional

The idea of the autonomous professional is one which seems to fit in with the private nature of classroom teaching. Indeed, in all our schools it was recognised that classroom discipline was essentially the responsibility of the individual teacher. As one teacher in Oldtown put it:

> At the end of the day the whole thing lands back on the teacher's plate. The system is there to investigate and expand upon that pupil's performance and actions in other classes. It can open it up in that way, but in the end the pupil will not be removed from the class in the long term . . . The classroom teacher has to devise a scheme of his or her own that works.

However, we detected differences among our schools in the extent to which teachers were free to define their own standards of discipline. These differences transcend departmental autonomy differences as we shall see below.

A department with extended autonomy may grant that autonomy in turn to the individual teachers in the department, to set their own standards of discipline. This was the case in some of the subject departments in Oldtown, as one assistant head of department suggested: 'I have no oversight of my colleagues. It's a level of impression [how they work] rather than a serious idea'. On the other hand, a department with extended autonomy may see each individual teacher in the department as part of a disciplined team following a standard pattern. In a different subject department in Oldtown, one of the staff said: 'I find it very easy to have it written down in black and white. It's rules that have been made as a department and I carry them through almost to the letter of the law. Obviously you have to. If you are giving out punishments, consider pupils' ability, but if they break a rule, you enforce it'.

The extended autonomy of subject departments, therefore, did not automatically mean that the individual teachers within these departments were free to set their own classroom rules and use whatever sanctions they thought were appropriate when pupils broke the rules. In some departments this did happen, with each teacher regarded as an autonomous individual within the overall framework set down by the school. In other departments, teachers agreed to operate by the rules and sanctions endorsed as 'the department's'. Within this extended departmental autonomy, the amount of freedom given to individual staff was justified on the grounds of promoting good discipline in the departments concerned. The chief benefit of individual freedom or individual constraint within a department with extended autonomy was that such freedom or constraint suited or helped the department.

The extended autonomy of subject departments also meant that there were differences in how heads of department helped a colleague with discipline problems. In Oldtown, various examples were cited of help given, accepted and welcomed, and of help given, resented and construed as interference. Of course, personalities entered into the equation, but it seemed that extended autonomy for the department made the sharing of problems something to be initiated by the head of department. Where teachers operate on a basis of restricted autonomy, it is easier for heads of department and senior teachers to offer guidance on classroom discipline, to team teach and generally to promote teaching as a shared rather than as a private activity.

Where teachers operated to departmental definitions of discipline and agreed to adopt similar approaches to promote good discipline, then the department could take precedence over whole school concerns. A teacher in Oldtown hints at this, in finding classroom discipline more vital than school discipline:

> All teachers are encouraged [by senior management] to appear at the classroom door and generally supervise, but it's not a rigid thing . . . With teachers being under pressure it's regarded as time-wasting. Two days a week I have no time off and it's enough to keep 149 pupils going through my head without having time to step out into the corridor – which then affects classroom discipline anyway. . . .

This could be a cost readily borne in a stable school with a minority of troublesome pupils and with a senior staff willing to take on responsibility for discipline in the public parts of the school.

Where departments operated on a basis of restricted autonomy, this meant that the individual teachers were expected to conform to the general consensus on how to promote and maintain good discipline. The weight of general expectations in the school, the similarities between departments in dealing with indiscipline and the open discussion of what counted as good discipline could all combine to put pressure on an individual teacher who was having discipline problems. There was the potential cost of teachers feeling somehow to blame if they had a persistent problem with an individual pupil or with a class. As one teacher in St James said: 'It's not the child that's at fault but your teaching. So it's not the child who is dealt with. You're perceived as weak by the class. It makes life a lot tougher'.

Nevertheless, the benefits of restricted autonomy within departments, for the individual teachers in Braidburn and St James, were seen as far outweighing the costs. These benefits were that the teachers tried to adhere to common expectations of keeping discipline, that the public part of the school was seen to belong to everyone, to be teachers' territory just as much as classrooms, and that problems could be freely and frankly discussed by most staff. At what stage a teacher's problems became labelled as persistent, and the teacher left feeling inadequate was not clear. However, it was clear that with open discussion and common standards as the basis of restricted autonomy, pupils were shifted to other classrooms if need be. Generally, this was on a short-term basis, 'to give us both a chance to cool down', but such a swap could be permanent. This seemed acceptable, defined in terms of 'personality conflict' rather than any inadequacy on the part of the teacher requesting the removal of the pupil.

Needless to say, in both Braidburn and St James there were staff whom colleagues saw as falling short of the ideal for one reason or another. Nevertheless, there was a belief that the whole school benefited through the pressures towards a common stance on discipline. In Oldtown and Easthill, there were common expectations in some departments, and difficult pupils were swapped about just as in St James and Braidburn. Similarly, some teachers felt it their duty to keep discipline in public areas of the school. However, differences between subject departments in these two schools made departmental benefits seem more central than whole school benefits.

Autonomy and pastoral care

So far we have concentrated on the different degrees of freedom granted to subject departments and the accompanying degrees of freedom for individual teachers. We have looked at what the benefits and costs of this were for school discipline in general terms. It seemed, however, that there were also benefits and costs in a very specific area, that of the operation of the school's guidance or pastoral care system. In all four schools this was seen as helping and supporting pupils with problems, not punishing wrongdoing. Most people in the schools would agree in theory with the definition given by a teacher in St James: 'Guidance has a difficult blend of being supportive and not being the person who gets you put out if you [the pupil] have done something wrong'.

Nevertheless, as we have tried to show elsewhere, the pastoral care system had a special role to play in helping pupils to conform to the school's way of doing things. The ways in which pastoral care was able to help 'problem pupils' were influenced by the kind of autonomy operated by the subject departments.

Where there was restricted autonomy, departments were seen as working in similar ways to promote good discipline and to deal with indiscipline. A problem with a specific pupil was seen as something that all colleagues could be consulted about, as we suggested earlier. This made it easier for the pastoral care team to negotiate with all the teachers concerned. The pastoral specialist could use this relationship of trust not only to work with the pupils but, more subtly perhaps, to work with individual teachers too. As one such specialist in Braidburn suggested: 'You don't take one side, you can't take one side or another . . . You have to try and work both sides to the middle, so you are allowing the pupil to see the teacher, and you are allowing the teacher to see the pupil in a different way or a better way'.

Where there was extended departmental autonomy, departments were seen as working in their own distinctive ways to promote good discipline and to deal with indiscipline. This made it more difficult for pastoral care to assist in dealing with indiscipline, in two main ways. First, they could not take for granted what counted as indiscipline in each department. Second, if the indiscipline was seen as relating to subject specific concerns, such as failure to do the work to the required standard, then the legitimacy of any pastoral care involvement could be questioned. After all, they were not necessarily specialists in that subject. One of the ideal roles for pastoral care in schools operating extended departmental autonomy, in the view of many staff, was to take 'problem pupils' away. This gave immediate relief to the teacher but, of course, did not make life easy for the pastoral care team. This view was expressed by a senior member of the pastoral care team at Oldtown, who felt that, as far as coping with a difficult pupil was concerned:

> Some teachers back themselves into a corner . . . Then when it comes to the notice of guidance, it's a straight choice between teacher and pupil, which to support . . . and if you don't support the teacher! . . . It's almost as if the teacher is saying [to the pupil], we'll make you commit this dire offence and get rid of you . . .

This applied with particular force in Easthill, where in addition to the pastoral care team there was a PSU with its own staff. Communication between the teachers and the unit staff was poor, and teachers expected that when a child went into the unit he vanished temporarily. One Easthill teacher felt indignant when such a child did not vanish; he reported that: 'Last year there was a boy put out of another teacher's room and he ended up in *my* room under the guise of the Unit.

In Oldtown, where the incidence of problems seemed low, extended departmental autonomy had in a sense affected pastoral care as a department. Instead of a subject-specific expertise as its hallmark, pastoral care had a recognised expertise in dealing with 'problem pupils'. Instead of subject-specialist knowledge, the pastoral care team had information about pupils and access to all the pupils' records. They were the professionals in dealing with non-conforming pupils. As such, and as a department, they were expected to do their work relatively independently. An experienced teacher illustrates this separationist viewpoint in her very tentative description of the role of pastoral care; asked whether the pastoral care team collected information about pupils she replied: 'I *imagine* so, but it would be a lengthy process'. The implication was that this was a specialist matter on which she was unable to make comment. She also said: 'Normally, I wouldn't hear about guidance dealing with a member of a subject class unless I read about it in the bulletin'.

If part of the work of pastoral care in reconciling problem pupils to school means that teachers have to be asked to think about how they teach, this can be very difficult in any school. Where departmental autonomy is extended, such advice could be construed as interference by one department in how another department worked.

The cost to pastoral care work in a school with extended departmental autonomy could be that the pastoral care team found themselves in a 'Catch-22' situation. To be trusted they had to build up their expertise, be a respected department – but respected departments were independent and did not attempt to affect how discipline was kept in other subject departments.

In this section we have tried to show that in our case-study schools the overall role of pastoral care was similar. It was to help and support pupils with problems, not to punish them. In fulfilling this role, the pastoral care team had to win the respect and trust of teachers. In the schools with restricted autonomy this was done by an open sharing and discussion of problems, as a pupil's problem potentially impinged on the whole school. In schools with extended autonomy, the pastoral care team tried to adopt the persona of a department. This gave them credibility, but it was more difficult to intervene in problem cases, where the problem was conceived as a subject specific one. We should add that, irrespective of the pattern of departmental autonomy, personal contact between the pastoral care team and subject staff facilitated the operation of pastoral care. Such personal contact may have been easier where subject boundaries were fluid but it was not impossible where departmental autonomy was high.

Conclusion

In this chapter we have described two kinds of autonomy. Extended departmental autonomy provided examples of good discipline defined in different ways by different departments. Where extended autonomy operated, the teachers in each subject department could themselves have considerable free-dom to set their own discipline standards, or they could agree to work to a set departmental rule book. Whichever approach was adopted seemed to be the result of agreement between staff within the department, and was justified as something which benefited good discipline in the department concerned. We have argued that the major benefit of this system was the enhanced profes-sionalism of heads of department. One cost was the operation of different standards across the school as a whole. Some pupils may have found it hard to adjust from class to class. Other pupils may have tried to play off teachers against one another, by claiming to stricter teachers that other colleagues allowed various rule infringements. Another cost was the prominence given to departments' discipline to the possible detriment of discipline in non-departmental areas such as corridors.

Restricted autonomy provided examples of good discipline defined in simi-lar ways across different departments. Individual teachers within these de-partments had necessarily restricted autonomy too. This was seen as beneficial to overall good discipline in the school, but the cost was a certain lack of freedom. Departments could extend their autonomy, but only if the extension was seen by senior management as a legitimate one. There were costs of restricted autonomy borne by the staff, especially in terms of demands about involvement in the overall work of the school.

The pastoral care team in all four schools seemed to hold quite similar views about their role in helping disaffected pupils come to terms with school, and about how they might go about promoting good discipline for all pupils. To make these views heard, the pastoral care team had to imitate the pattern of autonomy prevalent in each school. That is, where restricted autonomy was the pattern, pastoral care eschewed departmental status and emphasised links with their subject departments, their contacts and friend-ships. Where extended autonomy was the pattern, pastoral care emphasised their departmental status and their expertise, their official role as coun-sellors, their formal role of collecting information. Obviously, there were implications in both of these situations for benefits and costs to good disci-pline. The broad implications of extended autonomy and restricted auto-nomy are presented in Table 5.1.

As a final note, we should remind readers that each of these schools had a context and a history, that the autonomy of the school itself could be con-strained by outside circumstances, or even by ideas. In all four of our schools, staff would agree with the headteacher of Oldtown, who pointed out that 'social expectations change . . . The school has changed over the years'.

Table 5.1:   Benefits and costs: The amount of autonomy given to subject departments and to individual teachers influences whole school discipline

Extended autonomy	Restricted autonomy

HOW DOES THIS AFFECT THE APPLICATION OF SCHOOL RULES?

Rules are dependent on departmental policy.	Rules are grounded in whole school policy.

Benefits

<ul><li>It extends the professional responsibility of the principal teacher.</li><li>Individual teachers may be able to contribute to departmental policy.</li><li>The rule system accords with the kind of work expected from the pupils.</li></ul>	<ul><li>There is a whole school effort to maintain good discipline.</li><li>Pupils are aware of common expectation of behaviour.</li><li>Teachers feel secure in enforcing rules because they are supported by teachers from other departments.</li><li>Teachers apply rules outside the classroom.</li><li>Management can enforce common standards throughout the school.</li></ul>

Costs

<ul><li>Discipline varies between departments.</li><li>Public areas of the school are seen as less important than the departments.</li><li>Some pupils find it difficult to deal with different standards.</li><li>Management have to monitor the different standards throughout the school to check any wide variations.</li></ul>	<ul><li>There will be a threat to the professional autonomy of the teacher if the rules are not discussed with the staff.</li><li>Management will have to spend time persuading teachers to accept common rules.</li></ul>

HOW DOES THIS AFFECT THE APPLICATION OF SANCTIONS?

Departments can differ in judging at what stage to apply sanctions.	Departments are broadly similar in judging at what stage to apply sanctions.

Benefits

<ul><li>Sanctions can be gauged more readily to match the needs of teaching a given subject.</li></ul>	<ul><li>The pupils have a common standard of behaviour to meet.</li><li>It is easier for management to judge when to apply serious sanctions.</li><li>Teachers feel more confident because of agreement on sanctions.</li></ul>

Costs

<ul><li>The application of sanctions may differ across departments.</li><li>It is difficult for management to judge when serious sanctions should be applied.</li><li>Pupils may feel unfairly treated.</li></ul>	<ul><li>Sanctions cannot easily be tied to work.</li><li>The individual teacher is not so free to judge when to apply sanctions and for which offences.</li></ul>

HOW DOES THIS AFFECT HOW REWARDS ARE OFFERED?

Departments can decide when and for what type of behaviour rewards are offered.	Departments are broadly similar in when and how they offer rewards.

Benefits

<ul><li>Rewards can be gauged more readily to match the needs of teaching a given subject.</li></ul>	<ul><li>The pupils have a clear idea of what sort of behaviour merits a reward.</li><li>Rewards can be tied to behaviour as well as work.</li></ul>

Costs

<ul><li>The use of rewards may differ across departments.</li><li>Pupils may feel unfairly treated.</li></ul>	<ul><li>The individual teacher is not as free to judge when to give rewards.</li></ul>

HOW DOES THIS AFFECT THE PASTORAL CARE SYSTEM?

Pastoral care is seen as a distinct department, supporting subject departments.

Pastoral care is seen as a group of teachers with specific expertise, working with departments.

Benefits
- the pastoral care team is seen as having the professional skills to deal with problem pupils.

Benefits
- The pastoral care team is able to negotiate with teachers about the behaviour of pupils.
- Closer contact between pastoral and subject staff is likely to lead to common standards of behaviour.

Costs
- Pastoral care staff may have different expectations about pupils than their subject colleagues.
- Subject teachers may find advice from the pastoral care team difficult to accept.

Costs
- Informal referral may mean incomplete records of pupil behaviour.
- All staff must allow time for discussion of pupils.
- There may be pressure on staff to discuss problems with the pastoral care team.

Investigating school autonomy

How would you characterise autonomy in your school? What kinds of things do people say? Would you agree that different departments have different ideas – or do you feel that departments in your school tend to operate in the same way? The following suggestions are intended to help you focus on the autonomy you have and its relationship to discipline.

If you feel that departments tend to conform to overall standards:

- Think of an example when a head of department or a teacher challenged the conformity. What happened? What did management do?
- Think of an example when a colleague dealt with a problem in an unexpected or different way. What happened? Was this criticised or praised or glossed over?
- Think of an example when taking shared standards for granted led to confusion or misunderstanding. What happened? Who gave way, and why?

Thinking about these examples, would you defend or criticise the restricted autonomy in your school? What are the strong points with respect to discipline? Could you use Table 5.1 to identify weak points? How would you cope with these? Was the school able to cope with challenges posed?

If you feel that departments are free to set their own standards:

- Think of an example when departments were critical of one another's different expectations. What happened? How was this resolved?

- Think of an example when a new rule or sanction was introduced. Did departments reinterpret this rule? What happened?
- Think of an example when different standards led to difficulties for a pupil or pupils. What happened? Did management resolve the situation?

Thinking about these examples, would you defend or criticise the extended autonomy in your school? What are the strong points with respect to discipline? Could you use Table 5.1 to identify weak points? How would you cope with these? Was the school able to cope with challenges posed?

References

Dearden, R. F. (1975) Autonomy as an educational ideal: I, in S. C. Brown, (ed.) *Philosophers Discuss Education*, Macmillan, London.

Johnstone, M. and Munn, P. (1987) *Discipline: A Pilot Study* (SCRE Project Report), Scottish Council for Research in Education, Edinburgh.

6
A FRAMEWORK FOR UNDERSTANDING CLASSROOM DISCIPLINE

So far we have been examining whole school discipline policy and practice. We have looked at the different approaches among schools and summed up their costs and benefits. We now concentrate on effective classroom discipline and on the similarities among the teachers we studied. Although these teachers were different from one another in many ways – for example, they taught different subjects, had gone to different training colleges, had been teaching for different amounts of time, some were male and some female – they had a common approach to promoting classroom discipline. In general terms this consisted of:

- advance planning and preparation to avoid disruption;
- reacting to disruption or to threats of it by using a variety of techniques;
- using their knowledge of individual pupils and the class as a whole to select an appropriate method of discipline;
- being sensitive to a range of influences on their effectiveness, such as time of day, or the subject matter of the lesson.

Before looking in more detail at what the teachers did, we need to stress two points. First, we are reporting teachers' talk about their actions, not observation of their practice. This was because we wanted to get at teachers' own ideas of what was effective, rather than ask them to react to our observation of what seemed to work. Our approach was to try to understand what experienced teachers do routinely and spontaneously in their classrooms by getting them to describe and explain their approach. Second, we are reporting descriptions at a general level so that elements of our framework can be explained. Details of the kinds of actions teachers used and the various influences on these actions are in Chapter 7.

Choosing the teachers

In each school we wanted to study four teachers, as this number permitted contrasts and comparisons to be made but would not overwhelm us with so much information that we would not be able to analyse it properly. How were we to choose the teachers?

In secondary schools, it is relatively unusual for teachers to see one another at work and we speedily came to the conclusion that the way to identify teachers who were best at 'getting the class to work well' was to ask the pupils – the people in the classroom who knew a great deal about teachers' classroom practice. After some pilot work experimenting with various ways of collecting information from pupils, we asked a random sample of pupils in each of the four schools to write about two things. First, they had to write down the names of the three teachers in the school who were best at getting the class to work well; second, on a separate piece of paper for each teacher, they had to write about what it was that those teachers did which made the class work well. The pupils were aged between twelve and sixteen and around 150 pupils in each school were involved in this exercise. As Chapter 8 shows, the pupils took the business of writing about their teachers' practice very seriously and were able to identify various aspects of that practice with a high level of sophistication. We discuss the methods used to collect information about the teachers' practice in more detail in the Research Appendix (see page 129). For the moment it is important to make clear that pupils identified many more teachers than we could work with and so further choices had to be made.

Our first criterion was that of frequency of mention. We eliminated teachers mentioned only by small numbers of pupils, recognising that this was somewhat arbitrary since not all the teachers in any one school would have taught all the pupils in our sample.

Second, we looked for teachers who were identified by more than one age group. We were interested in understanding effective classroom discipline by the same teacher in different contexts, and teaching pupils of different age groups was one obvious way of getting at this.

Third, where choices still had to be made, we tried to select teachers from different subject departments. Of course, the small number of teachers involved would not allow us to explain any differences among them as due to their subject specialisms. However, if we were able to detect patterns across the teachers from different subjects, working in different schools, teaching different age groups, then these patterns would be all the more convincing because of this diversity.

Lastly, the teachers themselves had to agree to take part. They had to be willing to put up with a researcher in their classrooms and be prepared to give up time to talk about their practice. In one of the schools, one of the teachers selected on the basis of the criteria mentioned above refused to participate.

Our sample of sixteen teachers (four from each school) consisted of the following:

- four mathematics teachers;
- four science (biology and chemistry);
- three English;
- three modern studies;
- one history;
- one French.

Of these sixteen, four were principal teachers (heads of department) and one was an assistant headteacher. There were eleven men and five women. All had at least five years' experience.

It is clear that our sample of teachers was biased. We selected the sixteen on the basis of pupils' perceptions of their strengths in getting the class to work well. As Chapter 8 shows, the pupils identified many different things which teachers did. Had we used different criteria, such as examination results or truancy rates, for example, we would probably have come up with a slightly different sample of teachers. Similarly, had we used headteachers or advisers or the inspectorate to identify staff, the sample may well have been different. 'Getting the class to work well' was our translation into everyday language of what we meant by effective discipline. Our definition of effective discipline was 'the creation of an atmosphere which allows teaching and learning to take place'. We clearly could not ask pupils to write about teachers in those terms.

How was information collected about teachers' classroom practice?

There were two main approaches used to collect information about classroom practice: we observed the teachers with their classes and we talked to them about what they did.

We observed each of the sixteen teachers with two classes for a fortnight. For some teachers, such as those of English and mathematics, this meant observing a large number of lessons; for others, in the sciences or in the social sciences, fewer lessons were observed as the teachers saw their pupils less often. Observing the teachers with two different classes gave them the opportunity to compare and contrast their approaches, if they wanted, thereby helping us to gain a fuller understanding of the factors influencing their approach. Observing over a fortnight gave time for the teachers and pupils to get used to our presence and it also allowed teachers to refer to such influences on their approach as time of day or lesson length. The observation was unstructured and non-participant. We took no part in the teaching. We noted in general terms what the teacher was doing and what the pupils were doing, taking particular care to note non-verbal behaviour as the lessons were tape-recorded. The main purpose of the observation was to provide a record as a shared reference point for the teacher and the researcher to discuss.

As near as possible to the observed lesson, sometimes directly afterwards, or in the nearest break or lunchtime, we asked the teacher, 'What did you do to get the class to work well?' The teachers found this a very difficult question to answer. We were asking them to make explicit their routine, taken-for-granted behaviour in their classrooms. We had many requests from the teachers to suggest what *we* thought they had done to get the class to work well. The whole point of our approach was *to elicit from teachers their own constructs of what they did* and we tried to resist the many invitations and temptations to offer our own opinions. This meant that initial interviews were often very brief, perhaps five minutes or so, as teachers said all they had to say about their practice. Our only interview probes were 'Can you tell me a bit more about that?' and 'Why did you do that?' and 'Was that the same as in lesson such and such?' However, as time went on, the teachers gradually had more to say, perhaps because they knew they were going to be talking about their actions and so became more conscious of them. It may be, of course, that they became more expert at providing 'rationalisations' rather than 'true explanations' of their practice.

Building up the framework

The remainder of this chapter sets out the framework we have derived from analysing teachers' descriptions and explanations of effective classroom practice. The framework is grounded in what teachers do, not in what they think they *ought* to do or what they would do in ideal circumstances. In analysing teachers' interviews we discounted all general statements such as, 'Typically I would' or 'Normally I do' if these did not refer to the lesson in hand.

Because of the teachers' varied backgrounds and career patterns, we had to develop a framework which helped understanding of these potential influences on how teachers went about promoting and maintaining classroom discipline. This meant that the framework had to be at a general level. Chapter 7 gives specific examples of teachers' actions and the influences which impinged upon them. Here, we set out the elements of the framework; these are as follows:

- actions which are proactive and actions which are reactive;
- a sign or signs to provoke reactions;
- two kinds of teachers' judgements – whether to act and how to act;
- a range of conditions affecting teachers' actions;
- a range of goals influencing teachers' actions.

Each of these elements is described in more detail below.

Proactive and reactive approaches to discipline

When our sixteen teachers talked about their methods it soon became apparent that they did some things in advance of the class appearing in their classrooms. For example, they would make sure that they were in the classroom before the pupils arrived or they made sure, in a science experiment, that they had the apparatus set up before the lesson began. Such statements we called proactive because they were taken in advance of any sign that the class was not working well. However, these proactive approaches did not just apply to the teachers' physical presence in the classroom or to setting up equipment. The teachers also talked about their lesson planning: making connections with previous work done by the class, thinking through in advance how to explain a difficult topic and about what kinds of activities would interest the pupils. Proactive approaches can also apply during the course of the lesson where the teacher makes sure that the class knows what it is supposed to be doing in particular parts of a lesson. An example of this kind of approach was given by the teacher who said, 'I gave them a chance to ask me if they had any difficulties [before they settled down to silent work].' The teacher explained that there was, therefore, no reason for any pupil to talk out of turn.

Being proactive, then, means that teachers prepare things in advance, they do not wait for something to happen to prevent the class from working well before taking action. (Interestingly enough, the notion of being proactive as an aid to effective discipline has been identified by many other writers, cited at the end of this chapter.)

In contrast, some actions are triggered by a sign or signs. Here the teacher is responding to a cue that individual pupils, or groups, or the class as a whole are not working well. These responding type of actions we have called reactive. For example: 'I was very aware of one girl talking. She was playing with a mirror. I watched her for about fifteen seconds . . . She realised . . . and got on with her work'.

Reactions can provide positive reinforcement of good work as well as serving to deal with disruption, as the following example makes clear:

> They were actually behaving very well. I made sure they realised it because it was a good period . . . quite enjoyed that . . . And that contrasts very well with the times when they know they're in big trouble and the humour has gone. It's stern faces all the way.

This teacher's reaction to the class behaving well was to make sure the class knew it and one of the ways of transmitting that was to use humour.

So far we have described one element in our framework, that of teachers' actions. But there are many influences on the teacher's judgement about whether to take action and, if so, what action to take and it is to these that we now turn.

Influences on actions: conditions

The context in which teaching is carried out has a profound effect on what teachers do and on what they count as getting the class to work well. What works in one lesson for one teacher with one particular group of pupils will not necessarily work for the same teacher with the same group of pupils in a different lesson, far less for a range of teachers and pupils. One only has to think of the difference between teaching mid-morning on a Monday and last thing on a Friday afternoon to see the force of this point. Many writers have pointed out the context-specific nature of discipline and how far we are from being able to satisfy beginning teachers' demands for a recipe for achieving effective discipline. In analysing our teachers' comments, we were struck by their references to the context in which they were teaching affecting their actions, and it is this which we have called conditions. We have classified conditions into a number of categories (discussed at greater length in Chapter 7) and give here a few examples to try to show how they impinge on teachers' actions.

One of the conditions most frequently mentioned by our sixteen teachers was what we have called 'knowledge of the pupil'. Teachers often cited what they knew about a particular pupil as influencing their decision about whether to act and what action to take. Such knowledge might include awareness of the pupil's home background, his or her behaviour in previous years in the school or particular abilities. It is not suggested that teachers' knowledge about individual pupils was necessarily accurate or complete; merely that what teachers believe they know about pupils influences their actions in getting the class to work well. In the following example the teacher explains his action, having a quiet chat with a pupil, in terms of his knowledge of that pupil:

> He is very backward. . . . He tends to be the butt of many of the other pupils' jokes. . . . I feel sorry for the boy. I think he responds to a quiet word rather than a shout or a loud command. . . . I had a wee chat quietly in his ear . . . that unless [his behaviour] improved he'd be sitting beside me.

The teacher's knowledge of a pupil can also explain a decision to act differently when the same offence has been committed. Pupils X and Y had both forgotten to bring their books to the lesson. This was breaking a well-established classroom rule. The teacher decided to punish pupil Y and not to punish pupil X. He explained: 'Y is a rascal of the first order. There is lots of information about him. He's just at it. X is low ability, a nice wee lad. He has genuinely forgotten'. We will return to this example later, but it serves to illustrate the influence of a particular condition, knowledge of the pupil, on the teacher's decision about whether to act and how to act.

Another condition which influences teachers' actions is that of time. We have classified a variety of teachers' statements about time under this general heading: time of day, the time available in the lesson and the time of year, for example, are all included in this category. One teacher explained that she had torn a strip off a class about their poor work because there were only two weeks of teaching time left before public examinations started. Another explained, 'I basically just let them let off steam today', because it was the afternoon before the Christmas holidays began and it was acceptable to her that the class should be lighthearted and spend some time doing quizzes:

> Some of them vote with their feet and don't come back in the afternoon before a holiday. . . . For the ones that come back you . . . can do one of two things. You can

make them work, which will teach them not to come back next time . . . or you can give them a reward. So I usually use things like quizzes or charades . . . and that's what I did today.

There are, then, a range of conditions which influence teachers' actions and these influence both proactive and reactive approaches to getting the class to work well. Conditions are not the only influence, however. The final element in our framework is that of goals and we now describe what these are and how they influence actions.

Influences on actions: goals

In any lesson a teacher has a goal or, more usually, a number of goals. These are what the teacher hopes will be achieved during the course of the lesson or as its end result. The teacher can have goals for the class as a whole, for example, that they get through a particular piece of work, and goals for a particular pupil, for example, that she answers a question. These are discussed in Chapter 7. Here we want to suggest that goals influence the actions teachers take in getting the class to work well. For example, one teacher gave pupils a task to do as they were watching a video during a science lesson to achieve the goal that 'the video was productively used'. Another goal mentioned by many of the teachers is to encourage pupils to answer a question and not feel foolish if they get the answer wrong. As one teacher explained: 'I didn't want to say "No" [to the pupil's answer] because I wanted her to feel she could answer again. . . . So I said, "Well, it's not right but it's not wrong." . . . She was on her way to the right answer'. Another teacher stressed: 'I take daft answers as well as good answers because I don't like to discourage anyone from answering out'.

Goals can be in conflict and can assume different orders of priority. If we return to the example of the teacher who punished pupil Y and not pupil X for the same offence of forgetting to bring their books, we can see from the teacher's explanation that it was goal conflict as well as the influence of the knowledge of the pupil which led to his actions. Pupil X was an habitual truant and his appearance in the class was the first for some time. The teacher did not want to put him off returning to school by giving him a punishment on his first day back. This goal assumed a higher priority than the goal of wanting to be seen to be fair in his handling of breaches of classroom rules. Let the teacher explain the rationale for his decision in his own words:

> He's [Pupil X] low ability, an awful nice wee lad. We're lucky if we get him to school each day, so I'm bending the rules with him which is a bit unfair because . . . I didn't give him a punishment exercise . . . With anyone else I would have, but I felt it's so good to have him here and he has *genuinely* forgotten.

A few moments later the teacher makes clear that one of his goals is to be seen to be fair:

> You've got to bend over backwards to prove that you are fair, and very often you've got to explain things to pupils to make them aware why they are wrong. . . . I do try to be fair to them.

This single example demonstrates not only the complexity of the decision making – the teacher is having to make judgements about whether to take action, which action would be appropriate given the circumstances of the pupils concerned, and to make decisions about the order of priority of conflicting goals – it also demonstrates the rapidity of decision making. This entire classroom incident took less than three minutes.

The interplay of goals, conditions and actions

In the example quoted immediately above, it can be seen how a condition, knowledge of the pupil, influenced the teacher's goals and hence his actions. It is clear that conditions might affect not only the prioritisation of goals but the selection of particular goals in the first place. So, if a teacher is with a class of five eighteen-year-olds, all working towards scholarship level in history, one of the goals might be that the pupils should develop an understanding of historiography, or be able to discuss critically the role of the great man in history, or any number of so-called cognitive intellectual goals. On the other hand, if the same teacher is with a class of twenty disaffected youngsters about to leave school, the goal might be to keep the pupils quiet for the lesson. In our framework, the overarching goal, which we suggested to teachers, was that of getting the class to work well. However, as can be seen from the small number of examples already given, teachers talked to us about a number of other goals which they had and sometimes explicitly linked these to the perceived context in which they were working.

It is tempting to speculate that experienced teachers are expert at matching goals and conditions – in other words, that they know what are appropriate and realistic goals for a given set of conditions. It seems likely that they have a repertoire of goals which they can pull out as appropriate to the conditions operating in their classrooms. It also seems likely that when goals and conditions 'match', the opportunities for disruption are reduced – although, of course, the action which the teacher takes also affects the occurrence or not of disruption. Correspondingly, when goals and conditions are out of line, opportunities for disruption are likely to be increased. There are many questions posed by our information from teachers about what they do to get the class to work well. Not least among these questions is how teachers build up a repertoire of actions and goals and how they come to recognise their appropriateness in particular sets of circumstances. Some limited and speculative answers to these questions, generated from our sixteen teachers, are offered. However, first let us sum up the elements of our framework. These are:

- that teachers use proactive and reactive approaches;
- that reactions are provoked by signs (a particular class of conditions);
- that a range of conditions impinge on teachers' decisions about whether to act and how to act;
- that a range of goals influence actions and that goals can be in conflict;
- that conditions affect the selection and order of priority of goals;
- that conditions affect the achievement of goals.

We have tried to present our framework in a diagram (Figure 6.1) which we hope will help to show the interaction of goals, conditions and actions.

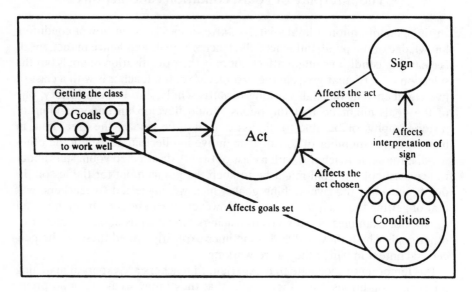

Figure 6.1:   How do teachers talk about getting the class to work well?

How do teachers build up repertoires of actions? As mentioned in Chapter 1, it is important to keep clear the distinction between describing teachers' classroom practice and explaining how they acquire the knowledge which informs their practice. The emphasis of our work has been in trying to describe teachers' practice in regard to discipline. In talking to us about their practice, however, the teachers sometimes offered explanations of how they knew that particular actions were likely to be effective. Our data are not as rich here as in descriptions of what teachers did. This is to be expected, since our concern was to try to understand what teachers did and the influences on it, rather than on how they came to acquire expertise.

Teachers' explanations of how they know what to do in the classroom to promote and maintain discipline tended to refer to their previous experience. They talked about this in general terms, finding it difficult to describe more particularly how they learned from experience. Typical comments were: 'Through experience you find your own way of working'. 'One learns techniques over the years which you find productive on both sides'.

How do teachers learn from experience? One way which we were able to classify was that of the past success of the action in similar circumstances. For example, one teacher who had sent the whole class out of the classroom at the beginning of the lesson because they were too noisy, and got them to line up again outside his door, explained: 'I did that because I've done it before and it worked'.

Some teachers, interestingly enough typically those in the sciences, talked about their initial training as a way of helping them to develop experience. They described how important safety procedures were in a science laboratory and that this had been learned in college. They occasionally made reference to the advice they had received in initial training on how to handle discipline. One teacher mentioned that students were always told in college not to say stupid things such as 'I'm waiting' because the pupils could always retort 'So what! You can wait!'

Our final classification of explanation for teachers' knowledge about what actions to take is that of beliefs about teaching. These beliefs were many and varied. One example serves to illustrate the general point. A belief mentioned by many teachers, and one which will be familiar to many, was that one should not ridicule a child for giving a wrong answer.

> [I think it is important] to be positive when they give an answer. I think it is important to reinforce, because they are 13 and they don't want to make a fool of themselves. . . . But that goes back to college training where you're told, 'You don't say "No", you say, "That's not quite what I'm looking for." '

Here we have a good example of a teacher showing how two of our categories of explanation interact. Her belief about teaching has been influenced by her college course and both of these are sources of knowledge to her about how she should act when a child gives a wrong answer to a question. Similarly, a teacher's belief that 'children like to be occupied productively' meant that he always tried to work 'at a good pace'. His knowledge of what was a good pace was built up by experience in teaching. Our limited data in the area of how teachers come to know what to do in particular circumstances raise intriguing questions about how experience and beliefs are built up. This is an area for further research.

How can the framework be used?

The framework is essentially simple and in many ways it would be surprising if it were more elaborate if it is an accurate representation of the concepts which teachers put into operation. The wide-ranging nature of the teacher's job and the unpredictability of the whole business of teaching would suggest that a complicated framework would not be workable in the day-to-day reality of classrooms. We have tried to show that the apparent simplicity of the framework camouflages the complexity of the decision-making in which teachers engage as they promote and maintain effective discipline. We have given brief examples of the wide range of conditions that impinge upon teachers' actions. We have given examples, too, of the different kinds of goals which teachers have and which may be in conflict. Finally, we have classified teachers' actions as proactive or reactive. It may be asked, 'How can we use this framework?' We believe that its main usefulness could be in the training of beginning teachers and in the professional development of probationers. We see it as being useful in three main ways:

- developing an observation schedule for student teachers to use when observing experienced teachers' classroom practice;
- helping student teachers to reflect on their own classroom discipline;
- providing a reference point for reviewing lesson planning.

Just as we are under no illusions about the difficulties of schools researching their discipline policy, so we are aware of the challenges of developing a teacher education programme which brings together school, college and student perspectives on teaching in a positive yet critical way. Our framework is offered as a contribution to understanding part of the experienced teacher's craft. Incorporating this understanding into teacher education programmes requires close collaboration between schools and colleges which go beyond the use of observation schedules and lesson planning formats. Our suggestions are intended as starting points for discussion.

Helping beginning teachers to analyse classroom practice

Beginning teachers are presented with marvellous opportunities to observe other teachers at work. These opportunities disappear rapidly once preservice days are over and so it is important that the maximum benefit is achieved from classroom observation. There have been many books designed to help students observe classrooms. However, these tend to concentrate on techniques of observation or on particular techniques of classroom control. They have not tended to provide an overall conceptualisation of what teachers are doing as they go about getting the class to work well. We see our framework as being a potentially useful adjunct to the classroom observation texts already available in providing such a conceptualisation. For example, groups of students studying a video of experienced teachers at work could be alert for the distinction between proactive and reactive approaches; they could be asked to note the explicit conditions operating in the classroom, such as numbers of pupils, seating arrangements, subject matter of the lesson and so on. However, they could also discuss any clues about implicit conditions from comments made by the teacher and pupils. There might be clues about the previous behaviour of the pupils, for instance, or the teacher's knowledge about a particular pupil.

Of course, there are severe limitations to the amount of useful information to be derived from classroom observation only. Talking to experienced teachers about what they are doing, and why, is an essential part of gaining access to their knowledge. Some recent research has shown the extremely limited time spent in conversation between student teachers and experienced teachers when on school placement. Clearly, structures need to be provided to ensure that there is time for both parties to discuss specific lessons. How can we ensure that if time is provided for such discussion it is rewarding for all concerned?

We suggest that a version of our approach to collecting data, namely asking teachers in an open-ended way what they had done to get the class to work well, may be a fruitful way of beginning teachers getting access to experienced teachers' craft knowledge. Our experience was that teachers gradually had more to say about their practice as the research progressed. It may be that one way of increasing the value of conversations between experienced teachers and beginning teachers is to use this kind of approach. Experiments in this have already been tried in Oxford and Glasgow which have provided some encouraging results. Much work remains to be done here, not only in providing the right structures to enable such conversations to take place but, more fundamentally, in teachers becoming accustomed to talking about the nature of their expertise. One of the most important elements in generating such talk is locating discussion in a particular lesson observed by the student. In this way teachers are encouraged to talk about the things that they did rather than the things they would like to have done. Clearly, it is also vital that students talk to teachers in a friendly and non-judgemental way if they are to encourage staff to talk freely and frankly.

Helping beginning teachers to reflect upon their practice

Many initial teacher training courses aim to encourage their students to reflect systematically on their classroom experience. Our framework provides one kind of structure to that systematic reflection. Students could ask themselves if they were proactive, for example, and if they became progressively more proactive during their school practice. Similarly, they could ask themselves if their goals and the planning to achieve those goals took sufficient account of the conditions operating in their classrooms. In essence, our framework provides one way of understanding the nature of classroom discipline. It is saying to new teachers that they do not have to rely on trial and error, or to see classroom events as 'one damn thing after another'. There is a pattern to the complex series of classroom events and in understanding that pattern they improve their ability to plan to get the class to work well. Contexts for such student reflection need not always be private. There might be scope to use the framework in the debriefing that takes place with fellow students after micro teaching. For example when they analyse their use of particular activities with small numbers of pupils in a safe environment. Alternatively, students could work in pairs in planning and analysing lesson plans before they go out on teaching practice.

Helping beginning teachers to develop their lesson planning

Research has shown that beginning teachers rely much more heavily on formal lesson plans than experienced teachers. The important point to make here concerns the formality of lesson planning by experienced teachers on the one hand and beginning teachers on the other. Many experienced teachers do not plan their lessons by writing out detailed aims and objectives, the time allocation of particular parts of the lesson, the key questions to be used, and the actions they propose to adopt – items typically contained in a student teacher's lesson plan. However, our data from experienced teachers reveal that sophisticated planning goes on in their heads and suggests that as teachers gain experience, they build up repertoires of actions and goals and become expert at recognising certain conditions as calling for particular goals and actions from their repertoire. The data suggest that experienced teachers not only have a repertoire on which to plan but also use the repertoire to adapt plans if things are not going well.

Our framework suggests a particular structure for the lesson plans of beginning teachers. It points up the need for students to be clear about the goals of their lessons, and this will come as no surprise to those involved in teacher training. It is already a feature of many colleges' pre-service courses. Our identification of a relationship between goals and conditions suggests that students need to be able to justify their goals in the light of the prevailing conditions, such as the age range of the pupils, the time of day of the lesson, the previous work done by the pupils, and their knowledge of the pupils. It would be unrealistic to expect new teachers to be able to make good judgements about the conditions affecting their teaching and so the regular class teacher becomes an important source of help. We see possibilities of our framework being used to develop a kind of checklist of conditions which beginning teachers could use in seeking advice about the appropriateness of their goals from experienced teachers.

Our simple framework of the key concepts which teachers use in getting the class to work well distinguishes proactive and reactive approaches to maintaining discipline. As mentioned at the beginning of this chapter, many studies have shown that effective classroom discipline arises from proactive planning. In other words, experienced teachers prevent opportunities for disruption arising through their planning. They do not wait for trouble to occur. This points to the need for beginning teachers to be as proactive as possible in their planning, not only because this is what experienced teachers do, but also because new teachers do not have the repertoires of actions which experienced teachers have to call upon. This means that if disruption does occur, beginning teachers do not have the same resources to deal with it. New teachers, therefore, need to be briefed thoroughly about the school and subject department procedures for dealing with disruption, the kinds of sanctions which are available and so on. Again, this will not come as news to those involved in teacher training. What may be news is the need to make explicit the rationale for all this information. This is not to make beginning teachers feel even more insecure than they do already. Rather it is to convey an understanding of the differences between experienced and beginning teachers in one area of classroom practice; to be seen to be providing practical support for new teachers and to make clear that experienced teachers are there to help. If both parties can conceptualise what it is they are doing in terms of the framework we have suggested, we hope they will be provided with a practical approach to making sense of one aspect of teaching classroom discipline. Crucially, we hope they will begin to see that the framework is a basis for reflecting on their practice and for helping their professional development as teachers.

References

Berliner, D. C. (1986) In pursuit of the expert pedagogue, *Educational Researcher*, September pp 5–13.

Brophy, J.E. and Evertson, C. M. (1976) *Learning from Teaching*, Allyn and Bacon, Boston.

Brown, S. and McIntyre, D. (1988) The professional craft knowledge of teachers, in W. A. Gatherer (ed.) *The Quality of Teaching. A Special Issue of Scottish Educational Review*, pp 39–47.

Brown, S. and McIntyre, D. (1989) *Making Sense of Teaching*, Scottish Council for Research in Education, Edinburgh.

Brown, S., McIntyre, D., Haggar, H. and McAlpine, A. (1989) *Student Teachers Learning from Experienced Teachers*, Scottish Council for Research in Education, Edinburgh.

Calderhead, J. (1984) *Teachers' Classroom Decision Making*, Holt, Rinehart and Winston, London.

Clark, C. M. and Yinger, R. J. (1987) Teaching planning, in J. Calderhead (ed.) *Exploring Teachers' Thinking*, Cassell, London.

Kounin, J. (1970) *Discipline and Group Management in Classrooms*, Holt, Rinehart and Winston, New York.

McNab, D. and Kennedy, M. (1989) *Student Teacher Talk: An Empirical Study of PGCE Students in Schools*, Northern College, Aberdeen.

Schon, D. P. (1983) *The Reflective Practitioner: How Practitioners Think in Action*, Temple Smith, London.

7
PROMOTING EFFECTIVE CLASSROOM DISCIPLINE

In Chapter 6 we set out a framework for understanding what teachers do to get their classes to work well and the influences on their actions. In this chapter we examine these issues in more detail. Tables describing these and the frequency with which teachers talked about them illustrate the relative importance of certain actions, conditions or goals for the sixteen teachers as a whole, showing:

- the importance of setting a clear framework for pupils by giving instructions and organising work so as to minimise opportunities for disruption;
- the high number of references to preparation and planning, class organisation, and explaining and helping children who were 'stuck';
- that teachers need to be constantly on the alert for detecting signs of bad behaviour and nipping it in the bud.

However, the tables necessarily underplay any differences among the four schools.

Within each of the schools we studied only four teachers and can scarcely claim that these four were representative of all the teachers in a particular school. Yet it seemed that each quartet made reference to the key ideas operating in their own school. For example, a key influence on teachers' actions was 'knowledge of the pupil'. In Easthill, such knowledge tended to be expressed in terms of pupils' negative qualities, consistent with the school's view of its pupils as socially deficient. An Easthill teacher might say 'You've got to watch Gary like a hawk. He has no idea what it's like to sit still for five minutes'. In contrast, in Oldtown 'knowledge of the pupil' tended to refer to academic potential and to be positively expressed, consistent with the school's view of its pupils as scholars. For example, 'You don't need to check up that Gary's done his homework. He's keen to do well'.

Of course, given the small numbers of teachers involved in each school, we cannot place too much weight on these school differences. They are suggestive, however, of links between whole school and classroom discipline policy and practice.

What do teachers do to get their classes to work well?

At the end of each lesson teachers were asked 'What did you do to get the class to work well?'. They made a total of 463 statements about the actions they took. The statements were grouped into fourteen categories and these are given in Table 7.1. The labels given to the categories have been devised by us. However, under each category we give some examples of the statements made by the teachers. We also indicate the number of references made to particular actions.

There are a number of points to make about Table 7.1. The first concerns the dominance of the category of giving instructions and organising work. This re-emphasises the importance of planning in order to get the class to work well and of minimising opportunities for disruption by ensuring that the pupils know what they are expected to do. We have already stressed the importance of a proactive approach. Of course, a straightforward listing of the actions mentioned by our sixteen teachers does not differentiate the proactive from the reactive. For instance, the comment 'I asked them to put their pencils down', could have been proactive, a prelude to giving instructions or to explaining something with which the whole class were likely to have difficulty; or it could have been a reaction to an unacceptable level of noise and the beginning of a verbal rebuke. However, an analysis of teachers' statements about their actions revealed that almost 59 per cent could be categorised as proactive while 38 per cent were reactive. The remaining 3 per cent of actions could not be classified unambiguously as either proactive or reactive. Thus the majority of the actions described by our sixteen teachers were not taken in response to a sign that something was amiss; they were taken to prevent opportunities for disruption arising.

The second point follows from the first. The small amount of comment relating to the actual use of sanctions is very small, only 4 per cent. This suggests that the amount of serious rule breaking was insignificant and that the teachers relied on a range of other actions to avoid trouble arising or to defuse trouble in the making. It is perhaps worth adding here that the sparing use of sanctions is borne out by our own observations. There were very few punishment exercises handed out in our observed lessons and very few occasions when pupils were sent out of the classroom. Of course, as many writers have pointed out, there is a hierarchy of sanctions which teachers can employ, ranging from a raised eyebrow and standing beside a pupil to the issuing of punishment exercises and detention. Among our teachers the use of sanctions

Table 7.1: Teachers' actions to get the class to work well

Category	Examples of teachers' statements N = 463	%	Category	Examples of teachers' statements N = 463	%
Gives instructions/organises work	I asked them to put their pencils down. I put the work on the board so as to organise their notes.	130	29	Gives warnings	I warned them what would happen if they didn't do their homework. I warned them that this part of the work would be more difficult.	24	5
Explains/helps	I clarified the marking scheme . . . and how they should have approached the exam. I tried to keep the introduction relevant to everything they knew.	50	11	Seating	It's quite deliberate policy . . . where I've got him seated. I spaced them (pupils) out.	23	5
Verbals/verbal rebuke	I raised my voice. I had to speak to him.	38	8	Uses sanctions	I kept (the pupil) in. I issued a punishment exercise.	20	4
Observes/positions	I stood at the front and observed (them). I sat among them.	38	8	Allows infringement of rules	I'm bending the rules and not giving him a punishment exercise. I didn't give Kevin a row (even though he'd forgotten to do his homework).	20	4
Reward/encouragement/praise	I gave (pupil) an 'A' for behaviour. I praised the efforts of the vast majority.	26	6	Uses humour	I made a joke of it. We had a bit of a laugh.	17	4
Uses normal routine	I used the usual procedures, books out right away etc. I reminded them about labels, the experiment, the usual routine.	25	6	Personal contact	I use their (pupils') names a lot. I told them a true life story about myself.	9	2
Asks questions	I went round the class taking answers. I tried to draw the answers from them.	24	5	Miscellaneous	I keep repeating myself. I lost my temper.	19	4

further up the hierarchy in terms of seriousness was conspicuous by its absence. Indeed, in general, most classes were happy and productive.

The third point to make is that there was a small number of comments relating to the teacher's mood. These statements included, for example, 'I lost my temper' and 'I was not happy'. It was difficult for us to know whether the teachers referred to these as actions which they took in order to get the class to work well, or whether they were conditions affecting the selection and use of other actions. Interestingly enough, the pupils also referred to the teacher's mood when asked about their teachers' classroom practice. On balance, we saw statements about the teacher's mood as being more appropriate as a condition affecting the choice of particular actions. However, we are aware that from time to time teachers do use their mood quite deliberately as an action to get the class to work well. Showing anger or disappointment spring to mind as obvious examples.

Lastly, non-verbal actions may be under-represented. A look, a raised eyebrow, a shrugging of shoulders, or a shake of the head were examples of non-verbal communication which we observed but to which teachers made little or no reference. Our method of relying on teachers to describe what they did may have encouraged concentration on talk.

The fourteen categories can be arranged into clusters of actions taken by the teachers, to show more clearly if there are patterns to their actions. Our view of clusters is shown in Tables 7.2 and 7.3. There are five main groups: Setting the framework; Responding to the threat of disruption; Explaining; Personal relationships/encouragement; and Other. Table 7.2 shows the categories we have used to produce these clusters.The distribution of teachers' actions across these five larger clusters of categories is also shown.

Table 7.2: Clusters of teachers' actions to get the class to work well

Cluster Title	Category	N = 463	%
Setting the framework	Gives instructions/organises work Uses normal routine Seating	178	38
Responding to the threat of disruption	Allows infringement of rules Observes/positions Uses sanctions Verbals/verbal rebuke Gives warnings	140	30
Explaining	Explains/helps Asks questions	74	16
Personal relationships/ encouragement	Reward/encouragement/praise Uses humour Personal contact	52	11
Other	Miscellaneous	19	4

percentages rounded off to nearest whole number

We have stressed the importance of being proactive to avoid disruption occurring. It is interesting, however, that about a third of the comments from these experienced teachers about getting the class to work well concerns dealing with disruption. This suggests that good discipline is not something that is established early on in the school term with particular classes and that is the end of it. Rather it is something which teachers work at constantly, reinforcing their rules and routines when the situation demands it. As the research for the Elton Committee showed, most secondary school teachers have to deal with minor acts of disruption every day. The research also points out that the cumulative effect of this upon teachers' morale ought not to be underestimated.

The general description of the clustering of teacher actions in Table 7.2 can be expanded into a description of the clusters as they emerged within the four schools. Table 7.3 gives this detail.

Table 7.3: Teachers' actions as clusters, for individual schools

Cluster Title	Easthill %	St James %	Oldtown %	Braidburn %
Setting the framework	35	30	39	55
Responding to the threat of disruption	42	31	21	13
Explaining	12	18	22	11
Personal relationships/ encouragement	8	11	14	17
Other	3	8	3	3

A statistical analysis of the relative figures in the various cluster categories would be ill-advised, given the small size of the teacher sample, but a suggestion of the differences between the schools emerges from the distribution of teacher actions shown in Table 7.3. For example, the 55 per cent of actions setting the framework for work in Braidburn may reflect the teachers' view of their own role as a guiding force. Similarly, in Easthill the view of pupils as socially deficient may be reflected in the preponderance of reactive rather than proactive approaches. However, with this exception and the small exception in Oldtown, the pattern over the schools is consistent from most often used to least often used actions.

Conditions

As we pointed out in Chapter 6, actions do not come out of nowhere. The actions used by the teacher are influenced by the goals which the teacher has set for the lesson and the conditions under which he or she is working. Let us now consider what teachers had to say about these conditions.

When teachers talked about the conditions affecting their work, they did not only mean the kinds of terms and conditions of service associated with the profession of teaching. Rather they referred to a whole range of influences which affected their decisions about the actions they took. As previously mentioned, such influences included their knowledge of particular pupils and their beliefs about teaching. Table 7.4 illustrates our categorisation of the conditions teachers talked about. As with Table 7.1, we illustrate the comments teachers made under each category. Teachers made a total of 528 statements which we classified as being about conditions.

Table 7.4 shows how dominant an influence the teacher's knowledge about the class and about individual pupils is upon actions. It is when we look at what 'knowledge of the class' and 'knowledge of an individual pupil' consist of that again we see school differences. In Easthill, knowledge of the class or pupil seemed to be knowledge of the class or pupil's negative qualities, of the likelihood of bad behaviour or disruption. In Oldtown, knowledge of the class or pupil covered likely achievement and skills as well as behaviour.

In fact, these two categories of knowledge about the class and of the individual pupil account for over 40 per cent of teachers' statements about conditions. It would be fascinating to be able to compare these data from experienced teachers, identified by their pupils as best at getting the class to work well, with data from beginning teachers. We speculate that beginning teachers would not make such an extensive reference to their knowledge of the pupils or of the class, simply because they would have been unable to build up such knowledge. It would also be interesting to discover if experienced teachers, but newly appointed to a school, referred to their lack of knowledge about the pupils and class as a handicap or an influence on their actions. We have stressed the dominance of these two conditions because we see these as having implications for pre-service teacher education if our data are at all convincing. Most notably, the data suggest the organisation of school experience and teaching practice so that student teachers have a chance to get to know their pupils. We return to this point at the end of the chapter.

If we group the twelve conditions into clusters we can see how dominant an influence teachers' knowledge and beliefs are on actions. Table 7.5 shows our grouping of conditions and their frequency of mention by the teachers.

Of course, any categorisation is bound to be somewhat arbitrary and we are conscious that we have grouped together rather different kinds of teacher knowledge. Indeed one might argue that some of our components of the general organisation category represents what other researchers have called, in a different context, 'situational knowledge'. What is clear, however, is the large number of different conditions which impinge on the actions which teachers take in the classroom. What is also clear is that learning about some of these conditions relies heavily on direct classroom experience. It is possible to learn about the differences between say, twelve-year-olds and sixteen-year-olds in general terms on the college component of a pre-service course. We would suggest that, in practice, this means promoting

Table 7.4: Conditions influencing actions

Category	Teachers' statements	N = 528	%	Category	Teachers' statements	N = 528	%
Knowledge of the class	It's hard to get them back once (their attention has wandered). If there's nothing for them to do there's a possibility of disruption.	115	22	The teacher's feelings	I feel sorry for the boy. I like to talk to the pupils.	22	4
				Numbers	This is a small class. There are small numbers.	10	2
Knowledge of an individual pupil	Garry is difficult. He's a boy who should be performing better.	98	19	External to classroom factors	Discipline is backed up by the school system. Government policy favours exams.	10	2
General working condition of the class	They were working individually. There was a test on.	88	17	Previous warning given	This pupil has been told off before. The class had already been told about chewing.	9	2
Beliefs about teaching/children	All pupils should be treated equally. Success follows upon success.	53	10	Teachers' past experience.	It worked with the 5th year (There was) a stushie (commotion) when they collected compasses themselves before.	6	1
The nature of the subject	It was a science experiment. It's a difficult passage this.	50	10	Other	There was a challenge there to do it correclty.	33	6
Time	It was the start of the lesson. There was time (to do it).	34	7				

and maintaining classroom discipline can only be learnt effectively by teaching twelve- and sixteen-year-olds and, crucially, as we indicated at the end of Chapter 6, by reflection on the influence of such a condition on actions.

Table 7.5:   Clusters of conditions

Conditions	N = 528	%
Teacher knowledge of class; of pupils; of the subject; past experience	269	51
General organisation working conditions of the class; time; numbers; external factors; previous warnings given	151	29
Personal feelings, beliefs about teaching or children	75	14
Other	33	6

Goals

As was evident in Chapter 6, the goals which teachers have for their lessons also influence the actions they take. Teachers have goals for the whole class and goals for individual pupils. A goal for the class might be to complete a particular piece of work; a goal for a pupil might be to get him or her to answer a question. Our teachers usually had more than one goal for a particular lesson but it was striking that these goals were almost always expressed in terms of what their pupils were doing. Brown and McIntyre (1989, p. 33), in their study of teachers' craft knowledge, identified a similar phenomenon:

> [Teachers'] dominant goals, and the terms in which they first evaluated the lessons, were concerned with establishing and maintaining what we call a *normal desirable state of pupil activity* (NDS) in the classroom. . . . The lesson was seen as satisfactory so long as pupils continued to act in those ways which were seen by the teacher as routinely desirable.

Brown and McIntyre go on to point out that what was seen as normal and desirable by one teacher could be quite different from the NDS of another. We have found this concept of normal desirable state helpful in categorising the kinds of goals which teachers talked to us about. Of course, we had already suggested to them one NDS, that of getting the class to work well. However, the teachers talked more specifically about what this meant to them. A couple of examples will give an idea of the diversity of the kinds of NDS which were seen by teachers as routinely desirable ways for pupils to behave. The first teacher conveys that his NDS of pupil activity during a test is complete silence:

Teacher: Well, the first thing I did was to emphasise that on this occasion, because it was a test, I wasn't going to allow myself to be [interrupted]. . . .The second thing, obviously, simply separating them out properly so that there's plenty of space between them.

Interviewer: Why is that important?

Teacher: In the case of a test you obviously need to minimise the effects of pupils . . . cheating but, secondly . . . these kids, if they are physically together they are simply tempted to talk. . . . I insist that everybody keeps quiet until . . . everybody has finished the test.

In the second example, a different teacher talks about her NDS of pupils' activity during a science experiment:

I asked them if there were any questions from them before we started and then I arranged their groups, reminded them about safety rules, especially bags and things in the passageways. I try to get one person out from a group at a time to collect things (and) to avoid any fuss. . . . I was at the front so that I was able to see if anyone was having problems then I was free to walk round once they had collected [what they needed for the experiment].

In this extract some of the teacher's NDS is explicit, such as the routine for collecting apparatus to avoid any fuss and being at the front of the class so that she could spot problems. Other parts of the NDS can be inferred, for example the heightening of consciousness about safety rules when experimental work is about to begin and ensuring that everyone knows what her or she is supposed to be doing to avoid confusion.

The final example of an NDS is taken from a history lesson where the teacher is talking about establishing an NDS with pupils she is taking for the first time. The NDS is that pupils know that they are in the class to work and that she is in charge:

I have to be confident of what I am doing and [be able to] give confidence to the less able [pupil] who is afraid of being in the class or maybe floundering a bit. . . . They need to know that I'll give them help. [I also want to give] confidence to the children who want to work [by demonstrating] that children who may think they can be disruptive can't get away with it. . . . It's a very traditional way that I have with the class, that I have them in rows . . . I wouldn't necessarily keep them like that all the time, but that is the way we are just now, so that they come into the class . . . with the idea that they are here to work and they know who is in charge. . . . I am the centre.

These three extracts give examples of the diverse nature of NDS and of the different actions which are taken to establish and maintain them. We were able to classify 204 of the teachers' statements about goals as NDS. This was by far the largest single category of statements about goals and can be thought of as encapsulating the different meanings of getting the class to work well. However, Brown and McIntyre also identified another goal which teachers had for their pupils: that they should make some kind of progress. Brown and McIntyre (op. cit. p. 39) make the distinction between NDS and progress in the following way: 'NDS involves something being maintained without change over a period of time; progress introduces a development aspect which contrasts with the steady state of NDS'.

They go on to distinguish three kinds of progress; the development of pupils' knowledge, understanding, skills or other attributes; generating a product such as an artefact or a performance; and progress through the work. We identified these goals from our data, too, but they were very much fewer in number than the NDS. We identified only 45 progress goals, compared to the 204 NDS. Brown and McIntyre do not quantify their analysis of NDS and progress goals, although they say that the latter were less numerous than the former. They were, however, talking to teachers more generally about what they valued in their teaching while we were concentrating on getting the class to work well. It is, therefore, not surprising that our teachers should talk more about their NDS than about progress.

As well as NDS and progress goals, however, we were able to detect three other kinds of goals from our teachers' statements. These are avoidance goals, reward and praise goals, and punishment and displeasure goals. They are mentioned much less frequently than the NDS goals and in many ways might be thought of as sub-sets of NDS. We discuss each of them in a little more detail below.

We counted 71 avoidance goals mentioned by teachers. Into this category fell statements about the purposes of their actions such as: 'to avoid them having to argue about it later'; 'so that I'd not have trouble later on'.

Both punishment and reward goals were very few in number. We logged only 11 punishment goals and 13 reward goals. Examples of punishment goals are: 'to show them that bad behaviour is never rewarded'; 'to show them I was not pleased'.

Reward goals included statements such as: 'I'm rewarding them'; 'to show them they had done well'.

The small number of goals in the punishment category is a little surprising given that almost a third of teachers' actions were classified as responding to the threat of disruption. This suggests two things. First, it reinforces our view that the kinds of disruption with which teachers had to deal were relatively minor. As already indicated, this is borne out both by our own observation data and by many other studies. The second point follows from the first: that in dealing with the minor acts of disruption teachers only rarely wish to punish pupils. Rather, their actions are directed at getting the individual pupil or the class as a whole back to the teacher's normal desirable state of activity. Again this is a picture which seems plausible. Our schools are not staffed by sadists whose aim is punishment for its own sake. Punishments are there to get the class to work well and it is in this sense that our data about punishment and, indeed, about reward goals should be understood. Alternative explanations, of course, are that teachers would not have revealed punishment goals to us, feeling that they would be unacceptable; or that pupils would be unlikely to identify as teachers best at getting the class to work well those who relied excessively on punishments. While we cannot be sure about the typicality of the teachers referred to us by the pupils, we are sure that in talking to us over the course of a fortnight's classroom observation teachers were not camouflaging sadistic tendencies!

We have spent some time discussing goals because we felt that these were more difficult to categorise than actions or conditions. In Table 7.6, we present a tabulation of the kinds of goals which influenced teachers' actions.

Table 7.6:   Goals influencing actions

Goal	N = 348	%
Normal desirable state	204	59
Avoidance	71	20
Progress	45	13
Reward/praise	13	4
Punishment/displeasure	11	3
Other	4	1

We mentioned in Chapter 3 different purposes of teaching and different generalised goals in our four schools. As a final footnote to this section on classroom goals, we should add that in Easthill, Oldtown and St James, the major categories of goal were referred to in an order which followed that of Table 7.6. That is 'normal desirable state' was the most important goal, followed by 'avoidance' then 'progress' goals. In St James, the last two took up almost equal percentages of the total description of goals. In Braidburn, the order was rather different, with progress goals being given far more often than avoidance goals. Again, the pre-eminence of progress goals in these last two schools seemed to reflect the strong belief of the headteacher in each that school can make a difference, and that the management of the school can carry this difference into effect.

The interaction of goals, conditions and actions

We began our research in the belief that effective discipline was highly context specific, that what worked for one teacher in one school would not necessarily work for another teacher in a different school. The data from teachers' classrooms and, as we shall see in Chapter 8, from the pupils seemed to confirm this. However, given our classification of actions, goals and conditions, we looked for patterns among them. Were particular goals associated with particular actions and conditions, for example? Clearly, the high number of conditions relating to teachers' knowledge of their classes and individual pupils suggested the salience of these conditions for teachers' actions and goals. However, the high number of NDS as goals made any kind of straightforward analysis difficult since NDS meant different things to different teachers. We can offer some limited impressions of what our data suggest but we should stress that these are impressions only and more work is needed in this area.

Progress goals, those concerned with developing pupils' skills, knowledge or the production of an artefact or performance, were typically associated with explaining and helping actions on the teacher's part. However, this reasonably clear picture becomes more blurred when we look at the conditions associated with these goals. Two examples will serve to illustrate the more general point. The teacher is describing a progress goal, 'to get the pupils to look on their own notebooks as a resource' in his science lessons. The action he took was to demonstrate to the class the way he used his own notebook as a resource. This action was tied to two conditions, his knowledge that pupils were not using their notebooks in the way he wanted them to (gained from observing how the pupils were working); and his belief that, in science, teaching notebooks were an important resource for pupils.

The next teacher describes a progress goal as getting the class to understand the notion of 'digging for victory' during the war. The action he took was to explain to them that they, themselves, often had to be encouraged to do something for the common good. This action was tied to two conditions, his knowledge that the pupils were already interested in the war (gleaned from their previous responses); and his belief that they would better understand the idea of the common good, if he related it to their own experience.

It can be seen then, that while there are some expected associations between actions and goals, the multiplicity of conditions surrounding goals and actions makes it difficult at this stage to detect clear, unambiguous patterns between all three. Furthermore, the complexity in meaning ascribed to an NDS of pupil activity means that any systematic search for patterns is fraught with difficulty. At this stage we see the benefit of our work as alerting the teaching profession to a framework for understanding how teachers go about promoting and maintaining classroom discipline and in filling out that framework by illustrating the actions, goals and conditions which were salient for them.

Conclusion

In this chapter we have tried to fill out the framework of teachers' actions, conditions and goals presented in more general terms in Chapter 6. We have stressed that teachers take a wide variety of actions to get their classes to work well and that these actions are influenced by a wide variety of conditions. Further, we have emphasised that what counts as getting the class to work well means different things to different teachers. Within all this diversity, however, certain points stand out:

- Setting the framework in classrooms to avoid the occurrence of disruption featured extensively in teachers' talk about their classroom discipline.
- Actions most commonly referred to were preparation and planning; organisation and management of the class; explaining and helping.
- Almost one third of teachers' actions were devoted to dealing with disruption.
- The kinds of disruption most commonly encountered were minor but irritating, such as pupils talking out of turn and forgetting books and materials.
- Reactions to disruption involved verbal rebukes, warnings and the sparing use of more serious sanctions.
- Teachers' goals were expressed in terms of the activities of their pupils. The most common goal was an NDS of pupil activity but this meant different things to different teachers.
- The conditions most commonly influencing teachers' actions were knowledge of the class and pupils.

In summarising our findings we should like to draw attention to the importance of the teachers' knowledge of their pupils and classes as influencing their actions. This seems to have two important implications for teaching practice. First, it suggests that student teachers need to spend time talking to experienced teachers about their classes and about the actions that are most successful with particular classes in promoting and maintaining discipline. Second, it suggests that there may be merit in student teachers spending their teaching practice in one school so that they can build up their knowledge of individual pupils and classes. It is not for us to advocate particular patterns of teaching practice. This was not the focus of the research. For example, we have no evidence to suggest that blocks of school experience juxtaposed with blocks of college experience are more or less effective than students spending part of every week in school and part in college. However, our evidence does suggest that our teachers rely to a considerable extent on their knowledge of pupils and classes as a guide to action in maintaining discipline. It seems, therefore, to be important to give students the opportunity to begin to build up this kind of knowledge so that they can consider it in the context of their more abstract knowledge about teaching and learning.

References

Brown, S. and McIntyre, D. (1989) *Making Sense of Teaching*, Scottish Council for Research in Education, Edinburgh.

Cumming, C. E., Lowe, T., Tulips, J. and Wakeling, C. (1981) *Making the Change: A Study of the Abolition of Corporal Punishment*, Hodder and Stoughton/Scottish Council for Research in Education, London.

Department of Education and Science (1989) *Discipline in School (The Elton Report)*, DES/HMSO, London.

Eraut, M. (1988) Management knowledge: Its nature and development, in J. Calderhead, *Teachers' Professional Knowledge*, Falmer Press, Lewes.

Wragg, E. C. (1981) *Class Management and Control*, Macmillan, London.

Wragg, E. C. (ed.) (1984) *Classroom Teaching Skills*, Croom Helm, London.

8
PUPILS' VIEWS ON EFFECTIVE DISCIPLINE

So far in our discussion of discipline we have concentrated on what teachers had to say. Their views, however, are only part of the story – though a vital part – in describing school and classroom practice and the influences on that practice. Pupils' views are important too. Any study of effective discipline needs to take into account how discipline is seen by those at the receiving end. This chapter describes pupils' views on:

- effective classroom discipline;
- school discipline in general.

In three of the schools, St James, Braidburn and Oldtown, the pupils themselves had some responsibility for managing discipline through a prefect system. The prefects would typically assist in ensuring orderly movement in school corridors and in pupils entering school for the start of morning and afternoon lessons. None of the schools had actively involved the prefects or other pupils in working out what the school rules would be. The emphasis was rather on explaining the rationale for rules and on the role of prefects in encouraging their fellow pupils to keep to the rules. However, prefects were not without some power and influence on school management. We came across one incident where a senior pupil had been sent home from school because of an extreme 'punk' appearance. The prefects believed this was unfair and petitioned the senior staff about it. Eventually a compromise on dress was reached and the pupil was readmitted. This was the only incident of prefect influence we witnessed but it is illustrative of prefects' roles and responsibilities that their course of action was perceived as legitimate and reasonable by all concerned.

Task sharing, monitors and special responsibilities are all seen nowadays as ways of making pupils feel valued and so less likely to be disruptive. The case-study schools adopted such strategies to some extent, by involving pupils in fund-raising activities for charities, for example, or having a pupils' council which, in addition to organising charity work, provided a forum for pupils to air their views on various aspects of school life.

What did pupils see as effective discipline? Were there differences in views among the schools?

How pupils' views were gathered

In each school, we asked two form classes from each year group 1–4 (twelve- to sixteen-year-olds) to write about classroom discipline. We wanted to concentrate on what they saw as effective, and on real teachers and lessons, not on ideals. We therefore asked them to write down the names of three teachers who were best at getting the class to work well and then to write about what these teachers did. We deliberately asked for three teachers, to explore the idea that pupils might have some sort of ideal or stereotype which they would repeat.

The 543 pupils involved in this exercise took it seriously and wrote thoughtfully and sometimes at length about what particular teachers did. Naturally, the information we collected in this way was less rich and detailed than by interview and discussion. There was no opportunity to probe answers, or to ask for further examples or clarification. Yet a clear pattern of actions emerged. The top action for getting a class to work well as far as pupils were concerned was the teacher explaining and helping them with their work, especially if they 'got stuck'. This was closely followed by punishments for misbehaviour. It seems that pupils find a 'carrot and stick' approach effective, though, of course, much depends on the context.

Approximately 4,300 statements were made by pupils. Analysing these was a difficult and time-consuming task. It involved building up categories of teacher actions from a sample of scripts and checking and cross-checking that all the members of the research team were coding statements in the agreed way. Twenty-one categories were eventually established. The labels given to these categories are our own. However, we have illustrated the kinds of comments (verbatim) made by the pupils under each category.

Table 8.1 shows that most of the statements made by the pupils were descriptions of teacher actions. Of course, such statements were made with varying degrees of specificity. For example, one pupil comments quite baldly that her teacher is effective at getting the class to work well because 'She helps you when you are stuck'.

In the same category of 'explains and helps', however, another pupil gives quite a sophisticated appreciation of an explaining and helping action on the part of a teacher: 'If someone doesn't understand something he stops the rest of the class and explains it again in case someone else doesn't understand it and won't say'.

Such descriptions of actions, from the simple to the sophisticated, were the basis of sixteen of the twenty-one categories. However, there were three

Table 8.1 Pupils' criteria of effective disciplinarians

Category Number	Example of Pupil Statement	Category Number	Example of Pupil Statement	Category Number	Example of Pupil Statement
1 Strictness	he is very strict	8 Class control	she keeps the class well under control	15 Teacher-pupil relationships	she likes us all even if we are bad
2 Shouts, threatens, warns	tells you you will get a punishment exercise for not being quiet	9 Explicit guidelines	explains everything, gives a lot of examples before we do the work	16 Praise and encouragement	makes the class feel as if they're brainy
3 Sanctions	if you do something bad he puts you outside the classroom	10 Practical management	settles class into complete silence, does things in order, eg people get rulers, pencils	17 Treats and rewards	if we finish our work before the others she would let us draw or do a word puzzle
4 Showing up	gives you a red neck	11 Amount of work	every minute of the lesson is work	18 Success in the future	(he tells you) you could get a job with good pay if you do your best in (the subject)
5 Does not allow talk	never lets anyone in the class talk	12 Homework	gives you plenty of homework each night	19 Humour	she gives you a good laugh sometimes so you just seem to do the work that is set out for you quietly
6 Allows talk	lets you talk quietly but not too loudly	13 Interest, enjoyment, variety	she sets work which is interesting and allows a little of everything, eg art, poetry etc in each topic	20 Mood – Miscellaneous	she keeps her cool
7 Absence of strictness	does not shout or give out punishment exercises	14 Explains and helps	she helps you when you're stuck at any subject	21 Miscellaneous	she is very good at arranging things

categories of pupils' statements which we felt were descriptive of the teacher rather than of what the teacher did. These statements were usually brief and were of the following kind: 'He/She is strict'. 'He/She is not strict'. 'He/She can control the class'.

It seemed that although the pupils giving such responses were not describing particular actions on the part of the teacher, we should not ignore statements which made up about 12 per cent of the total. We included in our category system these descriptions of what the teachers were like, even though they cannot be presented as part of the comments on teachers' actions. These general statements were categorised under 'strictness', 'absence of strictness' or 'class control' as appropriate.

The remaining two of our twenty-one categories consisted of miscellaneous statements made by the pupils. In re-analysing these, a clear category of statements about the teacher's mood emerged. Such comments could be positive or negative, for example: 'She is always in a good mood'. 'He gets very angry'.

We have shown this category of mood as a subset of 'miscellaneous' in the charts which follow but we are unsure whether a mood is an action. We do not know whether the teachers use mood to get the class to work well by pretending to be angry at some minor misdemeanour. Alternatively, mood could be more appropriately regarded as a condition, affecting the teacher's choice of actions and goals as discussed in Chapter 7. All we can say is that about 2 per cent of the total comment was about the teacher's mood, suggesting that, to a limited extent, pupils are sensitive to this as an influence on classroom practice.

The remaining uncodeable statements formed the category 'miscellaneous general'. This category included infrequently given descriptive statements about teachers' actions, ambiguous statements and unclear statements. Examples of these are: 'He is good at giving work'. 'He has authority in the school'. 'She is my favourite teacher'.

It is interesting that, in all, about 19 per cent of the statements made by the pupils did not describe what the teacher actually did. Instead they were descriptions of the teacher in general terms of strictness or control or in terms of the teacher's mood. This may say something about the degree of difficulty experienced by the pupils in describing their teachers' actions or be evidence of the importance of a teacher's personality to a pupil. However, we were encouraged by the fact that over 80 per cent of pupils' statements concerned actions taken by teachers in order to get the class to work well.

The range and variety of teachers' actions

Did any specific actions by the teachers dominate all others? The short answer is 'no'. We analysed the pupil data in a number of different ways, looking for patterns. The first and most obvious step was to add up the frequency of occurrence of the different kinds of teacher actions.

Table 8.2: What do teachers do to get classes to work well?
Years one to four combined in four schools
(No. of pupils = 543: No. of comments = 4326)

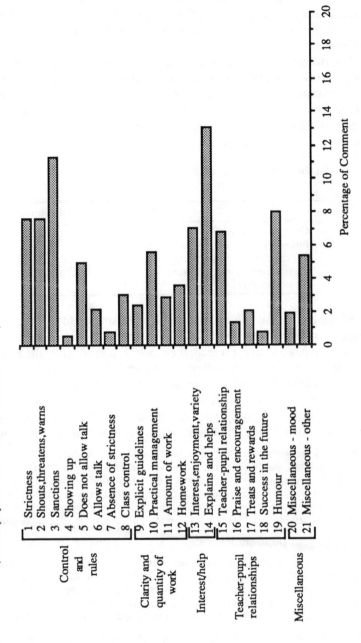

As Table 8.2 shows, the action most often given, 'explains and helps' formed less than 14 per cent of the comment. When we looked at the results for individual year groups in individual schools, some actions crept up to the 20 per cent mark, but no higher.

The overall impression is of a carrot and stick approach with setting interesting work, explaining and positive relationships being counterbalanced by threats, sanctions and general strictness. Table 8.2 shows the frequency of all twenty-one categories of teacher action. If we group these actions into clusters, is there then a cluster which dominates the others? We can see this more clearly if we look at Table 8.3.

Table 8.3:   Clusters of effective actions: pupils' views
No. of comments = 4326

	% of comments
Control and rules	39
Interest/help	22
Teacher/pupil relationships	19
Clarity and quantity of work	14
Miscellaneous	6

While control and rules form the largest single cluster, the more positive clusters of 'explaining and helping' and teacher/pupil relationships taken together are just as large. Overall, the teachers identified by the pupils as best at getting the class to work well used a variety of actions promoting good discipline by explaining and helping and generally having positive teacher-pupil relationships. At the same time they reacted to indiscipline by warnings and used sanctions as appropriate. A couple of extracts from pupils' comments give some idea of this range of effective actions. A first-year pupil wrote:

> She gets the work you have to do described to you in detail before you start and if you are stuck you will find that she always finds time for you. If someone starts causing trouble, all she does is give her/him a good talking to. If this person continues to cause trouble she just puts on a very tired, bored expression on her face and says, 'I'm just going to ignore you. I can't be bothered with people like you'. And, oh boy! you can be sure that it works every time. She never shouts at you.

A fourth-year pupil similarly described his teacher's approach.

> He always has the class working well and always has us all quiet during his class. He is always willing to help when you are stuck on a question. Some questions can be very difficult but he makes it look so simple when he shows the correct way it is to be done and often it's a lot simpler than I expected. He also likes a laugh but will not take any cheek from a pupil and soon the pupil will get to know this.

While the profile of actions identified changed slightly according to the age group of the pupils, some actions remained least frequently mentioned. 'Showing up', a West of Scotland expression for causing embarrassment, seemed to figure rarely. However, 'praise and encouragement' and 'absence of strictness', both more positive actions, perhaps figured almost as rarely.

It is also worth pointing out that some actions did not figure at all. As one might expect, advance preparation and planning on the teacher's part (our proactive approach), did not seem to be recognised by pupils, at least in those terms. Statements about making the work interesting and lesson management, however, suggest that pupils had some grasp of these activities. Indeed, there was a good deal of comment about interesting topics, books, plays and projects. The following is typical:

> She makes English enjoyable and fun for everyone. She explains every assignment we've got to do thoroughly and gives everyone a fair chance at everything. She treats us like adults and gives us a variety of work. We get drama, essays and lots of projects. We quite often have to work in groups which teaches us to get on with other people. She stands for no nonsense!

Perhaps more surprising is the absence of comments about fairness and consistency, given the reference made to this in the literature. This surfaced when pupils wrote about school and classroom rules, rather than in their descriptions of what teachers did. The few comments made on teacher actions relevant to these themes were placed in 'teacher-pupil relationships'. Finally, it is worth drawing attention to categories which directly contradict each other. A class can work well if the teacher does not allow any talking, equally it can work well if the teacher allows a little talking. Similarly, a class can work well if the teacher is strict or not strict . The pupils certainly identified a range of actions overall, but who were these teachers? Were the individual teachers chosen by the individual pupils because the pupil had some fixed idea of what a teacher should do?

Real or ideal teachers?

So far we have concentrated on which teacher actions were identified by the pupils. Now we ask whether individual pupils listed the same kinds of actions for the three teachers they identified, or whether they generated different actions for their different teachers. This is an important question. We need to know if pupils have a personal notion or image of a teacher who can get the class to work well. If so, then each pupil might see only certain actions as effective, thus identifying only these teachers who fitted the pupil's personal ideal.

As will be seen from Table 8.4, most pupils were able to generate at least two actions per teacher.

Table 8.4: Mean number of actions given, per pupil per teacher

	Year one	Year two	Year three	Year four
Oldtown	2.69	2.98	3.09	2.96
Braidburn	2.58	3.34	2.95	–
St James	2.32	2.55	2.49	2.83
Easthill	1.99	2.00	2.85	4.20

We looked more closely at the teacher actions given by individual pupils. Did each pupil repeat a pattern of actions for his/her three teachers? If there were repeating patterns, were they personal to that pupil, or were they common to groups of pupils?

For example, pupil 8 at Braidburn seemed to have some personal concept of an effective disciplinarian as someone who explained and helped and someone who used humour (our categories 14 and 19) as Table 8.5 shows:

Table 8.5: Braidburn, Pupil 8

	Actions	given
Teacher 1	14	19
Teacher 2	14	
Teacher 3	1	19

This pupil repeated a pattern of actions in his overall description of the three teachers he chose. However, this was unusual. Only eleven pupils used the same pair of actions, and those alone, to describe teachers as effective. Many pupils (310) used the same pair of actions plus a variety of other actions to describe what their teachers did. The remaining 222 pupils did not use any pairs of actions. They used a wide range of diverse individual actions. Our interpretation is that some pupils start off with a concept of what an effective disciplinarian is like, but this concept is expanded and fleshed out by their encounters with a number of teachers in secondary schools who use different approaches.

This idea was strengthened when we looked at the 310 pupils who used a consistent personal pattern (as well as other actions) to describe their teachers. There were very few repeats of patterns among these pupils. An example will make this point more clearly. Looking at the first-year pupils in one school there were twenty-seven who gave a paired combination of actions (plus other actions) in their descriptions of their three chosen teachers. Only one of these combinations was given by more than one pupil. It seemed to us that the pupils were choosing teachers not because they fitted some ideal but because of what they did.

Our next question is, did each 'effective disciplinarian' use all of the wide range of actions identified by the pupils? If not, was there a subset of actions which identified the teacher who was good at getting the class to work well? Or were 'effective disciplinarians' effective in different ways? For example, all the 'strictness' response in Table 8.2 may be descriptive of one group of teachers, while all the 'humour' responses in the same table may be descriptive of a different group. These are the questions we consider next.

Different ways of being effective

We looked more closely at the individual teachers, as they were described by their pupils. Between them, the pupils described about 70 per cent of the teachers in each of the schools. Some of these teachers were chosen by relatively few pupils, others by fifty and more. We identified twenty-six teachers in the 'frequent mention' category, teachers named by at least twenty pupils. Did these teachers use a similar range of actions? If so, we would begin to build up a picture of what an 'effective disciplinarian' did, as the pupils identifying these teachers came from different classes and different stages in the secondary schools.

Pupil descriptions of the twenty-six teachers provided different, although not unique, profiles of what they did. Most teachers had a peak action, for example, 'explains and helps' for one mathematics teacher, or 'teacher-pupil relationships' for one history teacher. These peaks did not displace other actions, even ones which might appear contradictory. For example, one teacher described as shouting and using sanctions was also described as using humour: 'He can take a joke. He jokes around with us and if you go badly out of line . . . he gives you a [punishment exercise]. He gives you a row only if you do something wrong. He doesn't shout at you all the time. . . . He is a good teacher. He gets on well with people'.

Similarly, another teacher who was strong on explaining and helping was seen as using control and rules actions: 'He keeps us quiet so we listen and are interested. Sometimes he has to shout or give out punishments so we quieten down so as not to get one. He helps you if you are stuck and doesn't let you struggle with things'.

None of the twenty-six teachers used every one of the twenty-one categories of action. On the other hand, none of the teachers used one category or one cluster of categories to the exclusion of the others. For example, none of the twenty-six was seen as effective solely by using 'control and rules' actions or 'teacher-pupil relationship' actions. Each used actions from the four larger clusters into which our categories could be grouped. The range of these teacher actions and the absence of a unique profile of the effective disciplinarian reinforce the view that the quest of beginning teachers for what has been called recipe knowledge about classroom discipline is mistaken. This does not mean that beginning teachers have to reinvent the wheel as far as action on classroom discipline is concerned. Rather, there is a range of activities which are possibilities to be tried, to be experimented with and to think about. These actions are not infallible recipes for success, because they have to be seen in the context of the goals that are set for individual pupils and for the class as a whole. They also have to be seen in the context of the conditions influencing teachers' goals and the effectiveness of particular actions.

Comparing pupils' and teachers' perceptions of teachers' actions

The sixteen teachers we observed, and who spoke about what they did, came from the group of twenty-six teachers mentioned by large numbers of pupils as effective in getting the class to work well. For each of these sixteen teachers we had their own views, plus the profile based on pupils' views. How did these compare? Table 8.6 shows a comparison of the top three actions identified by each group.

Table 8.6: Pupils' perceptions and teachers' perceptions of what the teacher did to get the class to work well

	Pupils	Teachers
1st	explains/helps	instructs, organises work
2nd	uses sanctions	explains, helps
3rd	uses humour	uses verbal rebukes/and
		observes, positions in class

As we suggested earlier, pupils may be less aware of proactive approaches such as organising work. A more immediate impact may be made by actions such as using humour, which appears to have struck pupils more forcefully as encouraging class work than it did teachers. There was an area of broad agreement between the teachers and the pupils who wrote about them. Both identified actions of explaining and helping, and of using sanctions or rebukes. This similarity gives some validation of our belief that teachers were able to explain successful classroom practice. Does this similarity also imply that, across schools, effective classroom discipline was more or less the same?

Broadly speaking the answer to this question is 'yes'. However, in Braidburn there were more pupil comments about positive pupil-teacher relationships than in any other school. This is further evidence of the emphasis Braidburn staff placed on the family/community aspects of school ethos and the consequent need to explain the rationale for rules and actions.

Before leaving the topic of pupils' views about classroom discipline we give some examples of pupils' comments about teacher-pupil relationships which illustrate the importance of feeling at ease with the teacher as an aid to learning. These comments come from more than one school:

When I came to [the school] I was worried about maths, but [my teacher] is quite young for a teacher and moves with the times and has jokes. He never loses concentration on the job he does but is very good and explains the work he teaches.

(First-year pupil)

She is a very good teacher. She puts over the message that she wants to know you personally. She talked to us like humans and not just kids coming to learn something at school. But if you don't hand in your homework or do something like misbehave she will really lower you down and you feel awful. She is very helpful and no one would speak back to her.

(Second-year pupil)

He is a cheerful and a nice person. He makes you work and if you don't know what to do he will come and help you. The thing I like most about him is he is a cheerful and kind person and also very helpful.

(Third year-pupil)

Pupils' views about school rules and sanctions

As well as asking pupils to write about effective classroom discipline we asked them to write about the school rules which affected them most, to describe an incident when rules were broken and what happened as a consequence. Most pupils did not distinguish school and classroom rules very clearly. School rules *were* the baseline rules in operation in all the classrooms. Furthermore, asking pupils to identify the rules which affected them most provided a similar pattern of response across all four schools. Table 8.7 shows the top three rules mentioned.

Table 8.7: Rules which affect pupils most
No. = 543*

Uniform/dress	325
Movement around school	229
Out of bounds areas	139
*Pupils could write about more than one rule	

The most frequently cited school rules were those affecting dress. All the schools stipulated in general terms what they saw as acceptable standards of dress and the vast majority of pupils criticised and resented these rules. The following comments are typical answers to the question, 'which school rules affect you most?': 'School uniform. I think you should be allowed to wear anything but jeans'. 'You can't wear what you want. You must wear a shirt and collar'. 'I don't like the rule that says we are not allowed to wear jeans in school. I want to know why we aren't allowed to wear jeans. It's not as if it's going to affect our performance in school'.

Movement around the school concerned rules such as 'no running in corridors' or 'the one-way system on the stairs'. These rules tended to be stated in a matter-of-fact way, with little or no comment about their fairness.

In contrast, boundary rules or rules affecting where pupils could and could not be at specific times were cited as irksome. They were seen as unnecessary constraints on pupil freedom as the following comments make clear: 'You are not allowed to sit in cloakrooms even when it is wet outside'. 'You're not allowed to stand inside the school [at breaks or lunch time]. What if it is very cold or wet or snowing? Have you to freeze or get soaking wet? You don't see the teachers outside. They're in the warm having tea while we are outside freezing'.

Boundary rules were a particular feature of the comment of St James and Easthill pupils. While all schools necessarily have such rules, pupils can feel resentful about the lack of social space, and common rooms and so on being available only to senior pupils. Of course, common rooms have to be supervised, cleaned and furnished – additional demands on schools' limited budgets. Given the importance of school expectations of pupils in affecting discipline and the positive comments about teachers who see pupils as people 'not just kids', it is an area of school provision which deserves analysis, debate and discussion.

As far as sanctions were concerned, the most usual response to bad behaviour was being 'told off' or 'given a row'. Most of the rule-breaking incidents which pupils wrote about seemed fairly minor and so the school's response of rebukes seemed appropriate. For more serious offences, being referred to senior staff and/or the involvement of parents were mentioned. Pupils tended to see such reactions as effective if the offender did not reoffend. An offending pupil wrote:

> I left the school without any permission and I was caught and sent to my guidance teacher. She put me on an attendance card and sent a letter home to my mother. Things turned out well because I don't go out of school any more and I get more education.

However, pupils also wrote about things turning out well when they felt they had got away with something. For example: 'Being told to stop carrying on in the corridor and after being told I carried on again but I was let off with a warning. . . . It was a good teacher and he had not stopped me before and so he let me away with a warning'.

The small numbers of pupils (less than 100) writing about school incidents which provoked the use of sanctions makes it impossible to generalise about particular schools. However, the far larger number of pupils who wrote about rules provided illustrations of the rather different expectations of their pupils held by the four schools. In Easthill, for example, pupils emphasised the negative, 'Don't eat in class, don't be late, don't be cheeky to teachers', which was consistent with the school's view of its pupils as lacking in social skills. Oldtown pupils tended to emphasise a positive formulation of rules, 'Be polite, be punctual, wear uniform, do homework and hand it in on time'. We would not wish to make too much of these semantic differences because a global view of the information from pupils suggests that those in the four schools had more in common as pupils than distinguished them as members of particular schools.

A pupil is a pupil

The pupils had a shared view of rules as being there to constrain their behaviour. Most of them accepted some rules as legitimate, especially those relating to work. So rules concerning punctuality, doing the work, handing in homework and being polite to teachers were generally accepted as a necessary and inevitable part of school life. Likewise, sanctions were seen as successful if they allowed people to get on with their work and if they were fairly applied. Rules on uniform and out-of-bounds areas were resented in all the schools, possibly because their relevance to a positive work ethos was not clear. Rules, for the sake of rules, were resented and pupils' sense of unfairness or injustice at not being allowed to wear jeans, for instance, was rooted in the belief that what you wore was not related to your school work.

In sum, it seemed that the pupils' concept of discipline was that it was a means to an end, the end being school work. It was not seen as a worthwhile end in itself. Comments about self-discipline being necessary in order for society to function were few and far between. The emphasis on discipline as a means to an end, implies that if school work is not valued as a worthwhile end, discipline becomes much more difficult to justify. It may be that our approach to collecting information from pupils, which focused on rules and sanctions, did not give pupils the opportunity to write about discipline as an end in itself. A question for schools to ask themselves is whether they see discipline as having these dual functions. If so, do they make both of these functions clear to pupils through their social education programmes? A key strategy for schools investigating their own practice is to find out what pupils think. Some ideas about how to do this are given in Chapter 9.

References

McIntyre, D. (1988) The transition from beginning student teacher to fluent classroom teacher, in S. Brown and R. Wake (eds.) *Education in Transition: What Role for Research*, Scottish Council for Research in Education, Edinburgh.

Marsh, P., Rosser, E. and Harre, R. (1978) *The Rules of Disorder*, Routledge & Kegan Paul, London.

Musgrove, F. and Taylor, P. A. (1965) *Society and the Teacher's Role*, Routledge & Kegan Paul, London.

Nash, R. (1976) Pupil expectations of their teachers, in M. Stubbs and S. Delamont (eds.) *Explorations in Classroom Observation*, Wiley, Chichester.

Nisbet, J. (1988) The contribution of research to education,' in S. Brown, and R. Wake (eds.) *Education in Transition: What Role for Research?*, Scottish Council for Research in Education, Edinburgh.

O'Hagan, F. J. and Emunds, S. G. (1982) Pupils' attitudes towards teachers' strategies for controlling disruptive behaviour' *British Journal of Educational Psychology*, Vol. 5, pp. 331–40.

Woods, P. (1980) *Pupil Strategies*, Croom Helm, London.

9

WHAT CAN SCHOOLS DO TO IMPROVE DISCIPLINE?

We began this book by stressing that there is no magic recipe for effective discipline. What works and is seen as effective in one school will not necessarily work in another. Each school has its own particular circumstances to take into account. However, we believe that our research has indicated some key areas which schools could begin to address if they want to improve discipline. These areas are:

- the school's expectations about its pupils;
- what teachers see as the main purpose of teaching;
- senior management's beliefs about its role in maintaining discipline, especially the views and role of the headteacher;
- the degree of autonomy given to subject departments and individual teachers to determine their own standards of discipline.

Although we have devoted a chapter to each of these aspects, they are all closely connected. We have separated them only to clarify them as components of that hard-to-measure phenomenon, school ethos. We can illustrate the interconnections by reference to one example, that of Oldtown. It will be remembered that Oldtown viewed its pupils predominantly as scholars, valuing academic achievement and success in public examinations. This view was operationalised in classrooms as teachers seeing the main purposes of teaching as transmitting subject-specialist knowledge to pupils who were willing and ready to learn. The primacy given to academic goals was evident in the extended autonomy given to subject departments to 'run their own ship'. Departments were the home of subject expertise and it was for the experts to decide what counted as acceptable work behaviour and good discipline in their subjects. This in turn influenced the approach to promoting discipline and reacting to indiscipline adopted by the senior management staff. The professional autonomy of the head of department was explicitly recognised, the pastoral care system was treated as a subject department and senior management involvement in dealing with indiscipline was low profile. Problem pupils were dealt with out of sight of the main school and a fairly strict system of hierarchical line management operated. So the whole approach had its own inner logic. The system worked in the opinion of most staff.

It worked because of the kind of school Oldtown was. Oldtown's history as an old academic foundation, the kind of pupils who traditionally attended, the low level of staff turnover, its physical location, and the expectations of parents about the schooling their children would receive, all combined to influence its approach to discipline. What a school expects of its pupils – or more generally, what its ethos is – is not a matter of unfettered choice. And changing its expectations or ethos is no easy matter. It can be done, though. Another of our schools, Braidburn, had turned itself round from having a poor reputation for discipline to having an excellent reputation. According to staff interviews this had been accomplished under a dedicated headteacher who undertook a programme of radical curriculum change, developed pastoral care provision, took parents, staff and the education authority with him and, above all, made pupils feel valued members of the school community. Such transformations do not happen overnight, of course, and the staff reckoned it was a good number of years before changes bore fruit.

Any school setting about improving its discipline is, therefore, undertaking a major task, which goes to the heart of the way the school sees itself. We say this not to put teachers off but to highlight the commitment and enthusiasm needed to bring about change and improvement. Writers on effective schools stress that there is no point in less effective schools mimicking the more effective by replicating some of their characteristics, such as displaying pupils' work or having homework timetables. These are the surface characteristics of a school's values and emphasis, which lie at the core of real change and improvement. The same point holds for school discipline. The four schools described in this book had their own distinctive approach which reflected their values. We have argued that each approach had benefits and costs, and that what worked in Oldtown would not work in Braidburn or vice versa. What does this mean for schools wanting to improve their discipline? First, real improvement will come about only if staff, particularly the headteacher, want it to happen. Second, improvement means more than cosmetic adjustments to rules, sanctions, rewards and pastoral care systems. These reflect a school's value system. Third, that schools need to make explicit their values and emphasis before they can change them.

What follows is a checklist of things to do to examine what schools take for granted about their approach to discipline. It is quite long and no school would want to pursue all these activities at once. One approach might be for an interested and committed group of staff to choose one area and see what they come up with. Another might be for the group to divide up tasks among themselves with a sub-group investigating the school's expectations of pupils, and another sub-group examining management roles, for example. The important point is that once the school begins to investigate its own practice it can see the extent of match and mismatch between intention and reality. It can then begin to develop ways of minimising any mismatch, perhaps by using the case studies in this book as a stimulus for discussion and debate, and coming up with its own solutions.

A checklist for examining school discipline

Expectations of pupils

- Read the school brochure as if you were a stranger. What expectations of pupils does it convey? Are these the ones you intend? If not, how do you bring about more than a cosmetic change in the text?
- Look at the school rules. Are the published rules seen as the really important ones? Do they signal expectations of bad behaviour by emphasising don'ts rather than dos?
- What messages are conveyed by the sanctions used for rule breakers?
- Does the school have any rewards for good behaviour or is the emphasis on bad behaviour being punished?
- Find out what pupils think. Ask a group to write about school rules, rewards and punishments.

Expectations of teachers

- How much freedom do teachers and subject departments have to set their own standards of behaviour? Find out by asking some heads of department, teachers and pupils: do not assume you know. Should there be more or less freedom? Why?
- Find out what new staff, probationers and students know about the school's discipline policy. Are they clear about rules, rewards, sanctions, referral systems and sources of support? Is the staff handbook helpful on discipline? If it needs improving, could new staff help with redrafting?
- Analyse the layout of the school. Are there particular trouble spots? Who is responsible for supervising these? Are all staff expected to deal with indiscipline anywhere in the school? What are the advantages and disadvantages of this?
- What would you say the dominant purposes of teaching were in the school? How confident are you that your view is shared by most staff? Check up.

Expectations of parents

- Analyse some recent typical communication from school to parents as if you were a stranger. What messages does it convey about the school's attitude to parents? Think about language register, tone, notions of partnership.
- How often do you communicate good news about the school, or about individual children to parents? Analyse the pattern of communication with a group of parents over a term with regard to, for example, year groups, complaints, good news,

fund-raising, welcoming involvement in school activities, sharing expectations about behaviour and asking for support before problems arise.

- Could parents be more actively involved in shaping and maintaining school discipline? If so, think about ways of involving the PTA and/or governors as a starting point.

Expectations about senior management

- Keep a diary of your own involvement in discipline over a week. What image does it convey? Is this the image you intend?
- Ask one or two pastoral care staff to keep a diary for a week about their involvement in discipline. What do these and your own diaries tell you about communication channels, feedback to staff, pupils and parents, and the extent of involvement of different staff in discipline matters?
- Find out what staff and pupils think about the role senior management plays in discipline. You could develop a short and simple questionnaire about this.

As we stressed, no school could undertake all of these activities at once. They are suggestions, ways of getting started. Some involve desk activities, such as analysing the school brochure or the school's communication with parents over a term. Others require active data gathering from teachers and pupils. The important thing is that they offer ways of challenging assumptions about the way discipline works in your school. Some of your assumptions will be well founded; others less so. When surprises and/or disappointments about the effectiveness of discipline are revealed, this in turn provides a basis for developing and improving policy. It seems that such an approach stands a better chance of sustained and real improvement in discipline than trying 'one damn thing after another'.

We have deliberately omitted questions concerning the adequacy of the school curriculum. Previous research has shown what a dominant influence on pupil behaviour this can be. Secondary schools now have to implement the National Curriculum and assess pupils' progress and attainment in accordance with pre-specified targets and levels. The view in Braidburn was that well planned curricular change, enthusiastically sponsored by senior management and by heads of department, had prevented problems of pupil behaviour. Changes in curriculum and assessment *may* have a positive spin-off in terms of pupils' behaviour, although there is no clear national evidence yet that this is so. In any event, schools are in the throes of large scale curriculum change and are already devoting energy to this area.

Our questions are drawn directly from our data and are designed to help senior staff examine what they necessarily have to take for granted in the day-to-day running of the school. We cannot suggest that there are right answers to these questions. We can suggest that, whatever the answer, there are benefits and costs, and we have illustrated these for the case-study schools. Staff in other schools might see things differently; much depends on the school context. We hope, however, that our analysis of benefits and costs of the various views schools held of their pupils, of the autonomy of departments and of different views of management, will help staff to look critically at their own school if they are concerned about reviewing discipline policy and practice. Fundamentally, of course, we have no research evidence from this study on *how* a school might set about changing its policies. Our concern has been to describe what we have called key ideas about the influences on whole school discipline. How to bring about change in schools has been the subject of a good deal of research and the literature has been reviewed elsewhere. Perhaps the main point to make and, indeed, the approach reportedly adopted in Braidburn, is the need to convince all those involved in the change that it is worth while for them, that school life will, in some sense, be better as a result of the change.

Three other points are worth making before leaving whole school discipline. The first concerns the role of the education authority. For most of the teachers in the case studies, the authority was a remote, distant entity. The authorities would, in fact, have had official policies on various aspects of school life which were not necessarily obvious to school staff. Teachers seemed to have very little contact with regional education officers, and this is not surprising. Local authority officers are few in number and it would be difficult for them to make contact with teaching staff as a matter of routine. They were available in times of trouble, such as when decisions to exclude pupils were in the offing, but data about the influence of the region on school discipline were conspicuous by their absence. The data were most voluminous in situations where the region was perceived as not backing up the school, when the school wanted to insist on school uniform, for example, or on the legitimacy of punishments for pupils forgetting school materials.

The second point is more difficult to relate straightforwardly to school discipline. This is the change which seems to have occurred in teachers' views of their responsibilities following the dispute in 1983 in Scotland. Staff in all our schools referred to this dispute and most saw it as deeply damaging. The move towards a contract specifying responsibilities has, in most of the schools we researched, led to a restriction of responsibilities teachers are willing to accept. In some of the schools this was manifested by a radical reduction in extra-curricular activities, which in the past had helped to develop pupil-teacher relationships. In other schools, although extra-curricular work had picked up again, teachers were much less willing to see themselves as responsible for discipline in school corridors and playgrounds. We have no wish to enter into a history of the dispute. We wish merely to point out that its effects were mentioned to us in all our schools and these were seen as detrimental to discipline. Clearly, any feelings of being undervalued, or not being trusted to get on with the job, will affect teachers' enthusiasm and willingness to examine school policy on discipline or on anything else.

The third point to which we want to draw attention to is that of school records on indiscipline. Each of the schools had its own system of logging indiscipline. All had a central log and most had a departmental log. The purpose of these was to enable a picture of a pupil who was behaving badly to be built up across subject departments. The logs were essentially there as a monitor of the individual pupil. Little use was made of them to compare the incidence of indiscipline from year to year, with the exception of numbers of pupils excluded from school. The use of logs to monitor the progress of individual pupils is another piece of evidence which suggests that indiscipline tends to be trivial, although irritating none the less. If our case-study schools were seriously concerned about a rising incidence of indiscipline, we could speculate that they would be using the logs to bring this to the attention of the regional authority or their unions.

Classroom discipline

Just as there is no simple recipe for effective whole school discipline, so there is no simple recipe for effective discipline in classrooms. Teachers, like schools, operate in specific contexts and the quest for an infallible list of approaches to discipline which would be equally effective in all contexts is, surely, a mistaken one. Information from pupils about the kinds of things which their teachers did to get the class to work well revealed a wide range of actions which pupils saw as effective. As we tried to show in Chapter 8, there seemed to be little consistency among pupils in their identification of effective actions by teachers. Pupils did not rely on one or two constructs of what counted as effective discipline. The teachers themselves reported a wide range of actions which they took to get the class to work well. What can we say, then, about how experienced teachers promote and maintain discipline in their classrooms? Does our research suggest that every teacher has to find his or her own salvation as far as discipline is concerned? The answer to this first key question is a qualified 'no'. There are ways in which our research on classroom discipline can help teachers. However, before we summarise these, it is important to be clear about what we are claiming for our findings on teachers' classroom discipline.

Can we claim that we have gained access to a part of teachers' professional craft knowledge? We are fairly confident that our findings do reflect teachers' professional craft knowledge largely because of the consistency of the accounts they presented. The sixteen teachers from different schools, different subject specialisms and different pre-service training courses talked in similar ways about their practice, ways which we have tried to represent in our framework of actions, conditions, signs and goals. They also endorsed our interpretation of their accounts when we fed them back to them for comment. Our confidence is further boosted by the face validity of our framework. It seems to make sense to other teachers who find it easy to identify with.

The second key question concerns the extent to which we have been able to map teachers' professional craft knowledge. Have we provided a comprehensive account of that part of craft knowledge which is concerned with discipline? The answer to this must be 'no.' This is because we have concentrated on what teachers do to get their classes to work well. Had we concentrated on how teachers respond to problems in their classes, then we might have got different responses. We can claim that we have been able to map a little of teachers' craft knowledge in promoting and maintaining effective discipline. How can this map be used?

We see its uses being at two main levels. These are more fully elaborated in Chapters 6 and 7. First, a glance at Chapter 7 will show the range of actions taken by experienced teachers. What is striking about this range is the dominance given to planning and organisation. We showed that well over a third of the actions described by these teachers related to what we have called 'setting the framework'. This emphasises the point made by many other studies, that experienced teachers plan to avoid the occurrence of disruption in the first place by making sure that pupils know what they have to do, and that the relevant materials are to hand, and by explaining the topic under consideration and helping their pupils to get on with their work. The importance of the establishment and use of routines was discussed by these teachers. The importance of being proactive is evident. We have also listed the reactions to disruption or to threats of disruption which these teachers most commonly used. These included verbal rebukes, warnings and humour. We indicated how seldom formal school or departmental sanctions were brought into play. In its own right, we hope our research will be of interest, especially as it emanates from teachers' own unprompted talk about what they did. However, there are many lists of tips for teachers in the area of classroom management and control. Is our classroom research offering anything new? Our answer to this would be a tentative 'yes', because the description of teachers' actions is embedded in a conceptual framework which tries to describe the many influences on these actions.

It is at this level of analysis that we see our work as being of most potential use. Any description of the actions taken by teachers to get their classes to work well is rather academic unless these actions can be embedded in the real contexts of classrooms. We have tried to do this by showing how teachers' actions are influenced by the conditions operating in the classroom and in the school. In particular, we have stressed the dominant influence on the actions taken of the teacher's knowledge about the class and about individual pupils. Furthermore, we have tried to show how teachers' goals influence their actions and we have highlighted teachers' emphasis on goals concerning pupils' activity, what has been called a 'normal desirable state'. Our framework for understanding how teachers go about maintaining classroom discipline, reveals, we hope, something of the complexity of teachers' classroom decision making. Chapter 6 illustrates the interaction of goals, conditions and actions and mentions the rapidity with which teachers make decisions. In Chapter 6, too, we outlined the ways in which our framework might be helpful to those engaged in pre-service teacher training and to those with responsibilities for probationers, as well as being of use to beginning teachers themselves. Briefly, these ways were: helping beginning teachers to analyse their classroom practice, to reflect on practice, and to develop their lesson planning.

We hope that by providing a conceptual map of the way in which experienced teachers promote and maintain effective discipline, new teachers can begin to make sense of some aspects of classroom life. Our framework for describing this particular aspect of the teacher's craft is distinctive in that it is based upon what teachers themselves had to say rather than upon 'espoused theories' or hypotheses about their behaviour.

Links between whole school and classroom discipline

There have been two main strands to our research on discipline:

- whole school policy and practice;
- classroom practice.

At the whole school level we have shown that there are key ideas which underpin whole school policy and which influence the way in which that policy works in practice. We have suggested that these ideas could be helpful in the field of school management training by using, for example, the costs and benefits tables and/or by generating discussion and practical exercises around the questions posed on page 32.

At classroom level we have produced a conceptual framework for understanding classroom discipline and a list of actions, goals and conditions which influence effective classroom discipline. We have suggested that the framework and the lists could be used in pre-service teacher education programmes and in helping beginning teachers.

It is tempting, but mistaken, to see these two strands of our work as separate. As we tried to show in Chapter 3, the school's view of its pupils is operationalised into the main purposes of teaching held by the teachers. These, in turn, influence the goals which teachers set for their pupils and so what counts as effective discipline in their classrooms. In Chapter 6 we showed that one of the most important conditions influencing the actions teachers took to maintain discipline was knowledge of the pupils. We also showed that there was an association between the knowledge referred to by teachers and the dominant school view of its pupils. Thus, where the school view of pupils was that they were socially deficient, then teachers tended to refer to the negative qualities of their pupils as an influence on their actions. Where the school viewed its pupils predominantly as scholars, teachers tended to talk about the academic prowess of their pupils. We have summarised what we see as the more explicit connections between our two frameworks in Figure 9.1.

This figure shows how fundamental the school's view of its pupils is to whole school and classroom discipline. Of course, our whole argument is that there are many influences on whole school discipline, such as how the headteacher and senior management see their role, the kind of autonomy

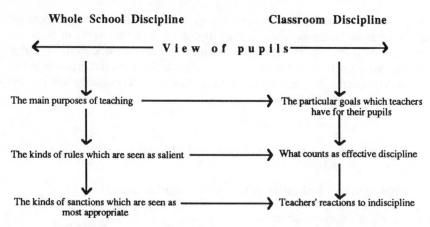

Figure 9.1:   Links between whole school and classroom discipline

given to subject departments and the role of pastoral care. Similarly, a whole host of conditions influencing classroom teaching is listed in Chapter 6. Our purpose in emphasising the explicit connections between whole school and classroom practice is to stress that school managers need to consider the possible effects of general policy on classroom practice and that beginning teachers need to be alerted to the influence of school policy on what they do in classrooms.

As in all research we are left wanting to know more. The further exploration of teachers' professional craft knowledge seems to be a fruitful way forward in extending knowledge about teaching. Questions such as the following all seem worthy of further research:

- How do teachers establish effective routines?
- How do teachers build up repertoires of actions to use in particular circumstances?
- Does subject-specific knowledge influence pedagogy? If so, in what ways?

Such research would be useful not only in extending knowledge for its own sake, but to contribute to our understanding of implementing innovations. Unless we know more about the nature of teaching we cannot predict whether innovations are congruent with teachers' classroom practice or so antithetical that they stand little chance of being adopted. Similarly, we can appraise teaching only if we understand better what it is. Finally, we can improve teacher education only if we know more about the teachers' craft. The current demands for schools to play a larger part in teacher training make assumptions about experienced teachers' abilities to describe their practice as well as about the ways in which new teachers learn their craft. Making the most of experienced teachers' knowledge means that we have to build on work already begun in the United States and elsewhere. Such knowledge needs to be elicited from experienced teachers, and grounded in actual practice if we are to understand better the complicated and multi-faceted business of teaching.

RESEARCH APPENDIX: RESEARCH DESIGN, DATA COLLECTION AND ANALYSIS

This appendix sets out in greater detail than was possible in the main text:

- the rationale for a case-study approach;
- the methods used to collect and analyse data on whole school discipline;
- the methods used to collect and analyse data on classroom discipline.

In addition, we include some information on failed attempts to collect data on classroom discipline from parents and from teachers not involved directly in the classroom research.

Before describing these details, it is important to make clear that the research was commissioned by the Scottish Office Education Department (SOED) as part of its policy-related research programme. The research questions were largely pre-specified although our proposal focused particularly on whole school and on classroom discipline to the exclusion of other matters of interest to the SOED such as the role of the regional authority in school discipline and the role of parents. Our justification for this was that whole school and classroom discipline were areas which teachers could do something about, were they so minded. These were areas which were more directly under teachers' influence than, for example, parental attitudes towards behaviour or social mores. Similarly, since the purpose of the research was to understand effective discipline, a study of deviant pupil behaviour or liaison between schools and the psychological or social services was seen by us as inappropriate. The focus of the research was on the approaches to discipline which were seen as effective. The main research questions are given on pages 4 to 5 of the text. It may be useful to remind ourselves that they concerned:

- what counted as effective discipline;
- the kinds of support available to promote effective discipline and to deal with indiscipline;
- whether indiscipline was defined and measured;

- the criteria used by teachers and pupils to identify 'effective classroom disciplinarians';
- how 'effective disciplinarians' operated in their classrooms.

The methods used to address these areas at a whole school level differed from those used in the classroom research. Before describing these, however, we say a brief word about the rationale for a case-study approach.

The rationale for a case-study approach

Our own (Johnstone and Munn, 1987) and other reviews of the literature on discipline (e.g. Docking, 1987) reveal the many different research approaches used to investigate the topic. These range from large-scale surveys focusing on particular kinds of indiscipline such as truancy, to case-studies of schools, classrooms and special units. Clearly, all approaches have their strengths and weaknesses depending on the research questions being addressed and the hoped-for outcomes of the work.

Our starting point was to understand why schools and teachers adopted their particular approaches to promoting and maintaining discipline. We knew that contextual factors were important in defining discipline and in promoting discipline but we had no clear hypothesis about which factors were important or about how factors operated. This ruled out a large-scale survey. A survey in such circumstances would have provided us with descriptive information about the policy and practice of large numbers of schools and t achers but it would have little explanatory power. Indeed, a survey could provide a useful general backdrop to more detailed work and also answers to questions about the salience of discipline as an issue for teachers. It could not extend our knowledge of why schools and teachers promoted and maintained discipline in particular ways.

Case-study work appeared to offer the possibility of uncovering explana- tions for schools' and teachers' actions. The case studies were at two levels, that of whole school (four schools were studied in depth) and of individual teachers (the classroom practice of sixteen teachers was researched). The possibility of explanation was provided by semi-structured interviewing about whole school policy and practice and open-ended interviewing about class- room practice. Case study also meant we could spend a considerable period of time in each school and get to know the staff, the rhythms of school life and observe at first hand the discipline systems in operation.

Clearly, the experience of four schools cannot be generalised in a statistical sense. Our identification of key ideas influencing whole school discipline and of a conceptual framework for understanding classroom discipline can be tested by schools and teachers interested in understanding their own practice. We see ourselves as providing conceptual and analytic tools for thinking about whole school and classroom discipline. We do not see ourselves as providing solutions for schools and teachers who want to solve problems of indiscipline, except insofar as we provide them with a place to start in understanding their practice and the areas to attend to in developing policy and practice.

Whole school discipline

Data collection and analysis : from teachers

A pilot study (Johnstone and Munn, 1987) had enabled us to explore the feasibility of semi-structured interviewing about whole school discipline. It also alerted us to the need to sample a range of subject departments. In each school we sampled teachers in the following departments as representing a cross-section of views:

- English
- mathematics
- science
- physical education
- art or music

Within each department we interviewed the principal teacher (head of department) and two other members of staff chosen at random. In addition, the senior management team and those with responsibilities for guidance (pastoral care) were interviewed in each school. Where feasible we also interviewed other professional staff such as the educational psychologist or social worker attached to any special provision for dealing with indiscipline. Table 1 gives details of the teachers sampled.

Appendix—Table 1:   Staff interviewed

Post in School	Region 1 (2 schools)				Region 2 (2 schools)				Total (4 schools)
	St James	Easthill	Gender		Oldtown	Braidburn	Gender		
			M	F			M	F	
Headteacher	1	1	2	0	1	1	2	0	4
Senior Management (Board of Studies)	3	2	5	0	4	4	7	1	13
Principal Teachers (Subject)	6	7	10	3	6	6	9	3	25
Principal Teachers (Guidance)	1	2	1	2	2	2	3	1	7
Teachers	8	10	7	11	9	11	10	10	38
Other professionals (social worker, educational psychologist, truancy officer)	0	2	1	1	0	1	0	1	3
Totals	**19**	**24**	**26**	**17**	**22**	**25**	**31**	**16**	**90**

Number interviewed in each school

The teachers were interviewed using a semi-structured schedule which covered the main areas of the research questions. There was a set introduction and ending but beyond this the interviewer tried to be responsive to matters raised by the interviewees and to use these to move from one area to another or to probe for more detail. All the interviews were tape-recorded and conducted in private. They lasted an average of about an hour.

All the interviews were transcribed and a coding frame was built up from the research questions. The frame was derived initially from a sample of interviews independently analysed by the three members of the research team. It was extended slightly on a subsequent sample and the initial sample was re-analysed using the new frame. Some data fell outside the coding frame. These initially were coded separately and some became 'core ideas' because of their recurrence and prominence in the transcripts. These core ideas became the key influences on school discipline.

A descriptive account of each school's policy and practice was fed back confidentially to each school for comment. The final chapter of each account was a speculative one based on the core ideas. Two schools had little or no comment to make, while the remaining two wished the accounts to be changed to reflect some minor factual inaccuracies and some matters of interpretation. Accounts satisfactory to both researchers and schools were achieved fairly easily.

Data collection and analysis: from pupils

Broadly, the same sample of pupils was used for whole school and classroom data. A total of 567 pupils, two form classes selected randomly from each year group year one to four, was sampled. (For details see classroom section, Table 2.)

Pupils were asked to write about:

- the school rules which affected them most;
- what happened when rules were broken;
- an incident when rules were broken and if the resolution of the incident was successful.

In three of the four schools this exercise was wholly administered by SCRE staff. Due to special circumstances in one school, form teachers administered part of the exercise. No significant differences in the data from the different kinds of administration were noted.

In general, the pupils found writing about school rules most straightforward. Descriptions of punishment systems and incidents were more difficult to analyse because of our failure to get pupils to distinguish between whole school and classroom events. More work needs to be done in this particular area.

The rules data were analysed according to a coding frame established from a sample of scripts, and independently checked. Each school's pupil sample was analysed as a unit. In this way we were able to establish a rank order for the most salient rules for pupils in each school. This served as illustration for some of the key ideas emerging more generally from the research.

Data collection and analysis: from documents

The ways in which a school presents itself in print were relevant to the research. Each school provided us with a copy of its brochure or prospectus, which was available to parents. We examined the format and content of these documents to find out if there were differences in emphasis among the schools about aims, rules, sanctions and the role of pastoral care. We were also alert for differences in the amount of information contained in the brochure. In addition, we noted any differences in the type and extent of extra-curricular activities offered and any mention of the involvement of the wider community in school affairs.

We also analysed staff hand books, induction materials for new staff and any policy documents for staff on discipline, where these existed. As well as noting the aims, rules and sanctions mentioned in these documents we were interested in references to the role of heads of department and of senior staff in promoting discipline or in dealing with indiscipline.

Where school or departmental logs of indiscipline were available we inspected these, together with records of numbers of pupils suspended. We were struck by two aspects of these. First, there were relatively small numbers of pupils suspended from school at the time we conducted the research. Second, the schools made very little use of their records to analyse patterns of indiscipline in terms of, for example, age and gender of pupils, times of year or subject department in which indiscipline occurred. This may indicate that indiscipline is a minor problem in these schools, or that a certain amount of indiscipline is seen as part of school life and not worth analysing or that schools have other priorities.

The analysis of all these documents helped to illuminate our ideas about the important influences on school discipline.

Field notes

In addition to the more formal research activities of interviewing, asking pupils to write about discipline and analysing school documents, we kept field notes about the schools. These were notes about day-to-day life, such as topics of conversation in the staff-room, the accessibility and visibility of senior staff, the ways in which any incidents of indiscipline were handled and the myriad other happenings that are part of a school. These notes helped to flesh out the views about discipline gleaned from other sources. They are necessarily less systematic than other data-gathering activities but have been used from time to time to illustrate points emerging from other sources of data.

Classroom discipline

Data collection and analysis: from teachers

There were two main approaches used to collect information about what teachers did in their classrooms to get the class to work well. We observed the teachers with their classes and we talked to them about what they did.

We observed each of the sixteen teachers with two different classes for a fortnight. For some teachers, such as those of English and mathematics, this meant observing a large number of lessons; for others, in the sciences or in the social subjects, fewer lessons were observed as the teachers saw their pupils less often. Observing the teachers with two different classes gave them the opportunity to compare and contrast their approaches, if they wanted, thereby helping us to gain a fuller understanding of the factors influencing their approach. Observing over a fortnight gave time for the teachers and pupils to get used to our presence and it also allowed teachers to refer to such influences on their approach as time of day or lesson length. The observation was unstructured and non-participant. We took no part in the teaching. We noted in general terms what the teacher was doing and what the pupils were doing (Walker and Adelman, 1987) taking particular care to note non-verbal behaviour, as the lessons were tape-recorded, the teacher wearing a radio microphone. The main purpose of the observation was to provide a record as a shared reference point for the teacher and the researcher to discuss. The teachers had access to the tape-recordings and observation notes, if they wished, as a means of stimulating their memory of the lesson. Few teachers used these. Most interviews were carried out immediately after the observed lesson and the teachers perhaps felt their memories of their teaching did not need refreshing.

As near as possible to the observed lesson, sometimes directly afterwards, sometimes in the nearest break or lunchtime, we asked the teacher, 'What did you do to get the class to work well?' The teachers found this a very difficult question to answer. We were asking them to make explicit their routine, taken-for-granted behaviour in their classrooms. We had many requests to suggest what *we* thought teachers had done, but the whole point of our approach was *to elicit their own constructs of what they did*. This meant that initial interviews were often very brief, perhaps five minutes or so, as teachers said all they had to say about their practice. Our only probes were, 'Can you tell me a bit more about that?' and 'Why did you do that?' and 'Was that the same as in lesson such and such?' However, as time went on, the teachers gradually had more to say, perhaps because they knew they were going to be talking about their actions and so became more conscious of them. It may be, of course, that they became more expert at providing 'rationalisations' rather than 'true explanations' of their practice. Our approach to collecting and analysing the information about teachers' classroom practice closely mirrors that of Brown and McIntyre (1988) in their study of teachers' professional craft knowledge, and we say more about our analysis of the data below.

Data analysis

In analysing the data we tried to follow the same procedure as that adopted by Brown and McIntyre (1988). This involved the following sequence:

- analysing (independently) a pair of teachers' interview transcripts;
- identifying their actions for promoting and maintaining discipline at a descriptive level;
- generating concepts which helped to illuminate the teachers' comments about actions;
- re-analysing the transcripts using the concepts;
- identifying the data not covered by the concepts;
- moving on to the next teachers' transcripts and using the concepts;
- identifying their actions for promoting and maintaining discipline;
- trying out the concepts previously generated, and so on.

This procedure was used for all transcripts. As can be imagined, it was a time-consuming process but one which would, we hoped, generate hypotheses to be carried from one teacher interview to the next. There was a good deal of brainstorming, of bouncing ideas off one another, and it was very important to have at least three researchers involved in the work so that concepts could be debated and rejected, or affirmed. The generalisations which we were able to establish as a result of this process were seen as providing the basis for the theoretical framework in Chapter 6. However, in generating this framework, we are, again, indebted to Brown and McIntyre (1988) for their identification of the criteria which had to be met in order for the theoretical framework to count as grounded in the data. These criteria were as follows:

- all aspects of the framework had to be directly supported by evidence (it is easy to add key elements which create a coherent abstract system but are not themselves observable in the data);
- the generalisations had to relate to normal practice, not to what the teacher did on rare occasions;
- where the generalisations went beyond one person and one occasion, they had to be based on data for each teacher and from each of that teacher's lessons;
- it was not sufficient to identify a series of generalisable but isolated elements as what teachers know or think, the relationships between these elements had to be identified;
- the framework should not discount any part of the teacher's account as 'diverging from relevant matters';
- the theoretical account of the teacher's knowledge and thinking had to be accepted by the teacher as balanced and adequate.

These demanding criteria were difficult to meet in full. For example, some data were excluded from our analysis because the interviewer had led the respondents, from time to time, by suggesting to them particular actions for maintaining discipline. Sometimes teachers talked about their ideal behaviour rather than their actual behaviour and these data, too, were discounted, although we made use of them outside the generation of a conceptual framework to speculate about how teachers come to acquire their routines and repertoires of actions.

When we had constructed the conceptual framework, we fed this back to the sixteen teachers, with a brief explanatory paper. Each element of the framework was illustrated by quotations from the teachers, and each teacher was represented more than once in these quotations. None of the teachers felt that the framework misrepresented what he or she had said. This endorsement, together with the consistency of the accounts presented by these teachers from four different schools, different subject specialisms and different pre-service training, gave us confidence that the framework accessed a part of teachers' craft knowledge. We should add that the conceptual framework has been discussed with several different teacher groups, who have found it easy to identify with, and who feel that it makes sense. We find a degree of face validity in this reaction.

Data collection and analysis: from pupils

In each school we asked two form classes from each year, year one to four, chosen at random, to do the following:

- write down the names of three teachers who were best at getting the class to work well;
- write on a separate sheet of paper for each teacher what he or she did that made the class work well.

Earlier piloting of a range of approaches to collecting data from pupils convinced us that writing was the most productive and economical way of eliciting this information. We had experimented with interviewing pupils singly and in groups and found this rather unproductive. Pupils are probably not accustomed to talking about their teachers' classroom practice to outsiders and we found it difficult to get pupils to talk extensively. We were more successful in encouraging them to talk after they had written about their teachers' practice. However, the amount and quality of this interview data were insufficient to justify the time demands of collecting it.

We had piloted different kinds of wording for the writing task and 'work well' emerged as the phrase which did not necessarily limit pupils to gross control and rule enforcement actions on the teacher's part.

Appendix—Table 2:   Number of pupils writing about teachers' classroom practice

	Year one	Year two	Year three	Year four	Total
Oldtown	59	42	46	37	184
Braidburn	56	30	39	–	125
St James	35	38	34	26	133
Easthill*	39	40	12	10	101
Total	189	150	131	73	543

*At the time of administration, these pupils had recently moved into the next year

The number of pupils from each school and year is shown in Table 2. In all but one sample of pupils, a sub-set of fourteen-year-olds in one school, the administration of the writing exercise was carried out by the research team. The sub-set was administered by form teachers due to special circumstances in the school. The overwhelming majority of pupils took the writing task seriously. Some wrote at great length and most needed the forty-five minutes set aside for the task.

The data were analysed by building up a coding frame from a random sample of scripts. Having established the coding frame among the three members of the team, the scripts and frame were given to an outsider to analyse. Eventually, after some amendment and debate, twenty-one categories of teachers' actions were established, with coding rules for each category. A list of all 'doubtfuls' and 'don't fits' was kept. The 'don't fits' were coded as miscellaneous if their frequency did not justify another category. 'Doubtfuls' were debated and assigned an eventual category on the basis of a group decision.

The coding was time-consuming. We identified over 4,300 statements from pupils about their teachers' actions. We continued to bring in an outsider to check a sample of our coding to prevent errors and keep the coding team on its toes.

The data from pupils are reported in Chapter 8. They were also used to choose the sixteen teachers whose classroom practice we studied. We chose the teachers on three criteria:

- frequency of mention by pupils;
- identification by different age groups of pupils;
- subject specialism.

As Chapter 6 indicates, the sixteen teachers (four from each school) consisted of the following:

- four mathematics;
- four science (biology and chemistry);
- three English;
- three modern studies (contemporary history and politics);
- one history;
- one French.

All had at least five years' experience.

Classroom rules: the pupil data

As we have already explained, the same sample of pupils was used to provide whole school and classroom data. These pupils wrote about school rules, classroom rules, and teachers who were good at getting the class to work well. In relation to classroom rules, pupils were asked to write about:

- the classroom rules which affected them most;
- what happened when rules were broken;
- an incident when rules were broken and if the resolution of the incident was successful.

This was an area of pupil response which was rather confused; some of the pupil replies about school rules had described classroom rules. These were rules seen as explicable to all classrooms in the school. Some of the pupil replies about classroom rules therefore repeated or expanded incidents already given as relevant to school rules. Other pupils omitted this part of the questionnaire. This meant that the data were difficult to analyse. Some pupil scripts had to be discarded in part at least.

Nevertheless, the classroom rules data were analysed according to a coding frame established from a sample of scripts, and independently checked. Each school's pupil sample was analysed as a unit. In this way we were able to establish a rank order for the most salient rules for pupils in each school. This served as illustration for some of the key ideas emerging more generally from the research.

Failed measures: teachers and parents

One area of the research in which we made little progress was in discovering the criteria used by fellow teachers and by parents to identify effective disciplinarians. The whole thrust of our research into effective disciplinarians depended upon the identification of real teachers. We did not want to create another list of traits ascribed in an ideal world to a hypothetical effective disciplinarian. The pupils had been able to name such teachers and to describe what they did to get the class to work well. We hoped to compare and contrast these criteria with those used by teachers and parents.

In the first two of our case-study schools we asked teachers to write about what their colleagues did to get classes to work well. We piloted such a measure successfully on an admittedly small group of teachers, but this was done outside their schools. This proved an important condition. In one of our schools, teachers saw the measure as disguised appraisal, and we were advised not to proceed. In the other school, the measure was distributed via staff pigeonholes. The researchers tried to encourage teachers to complete the measure, which was to be returned in sealed envelopes. In the event, twelve forms were returned of sixty-two distributed – and seven of these were not completed save for an apologetic or irate message.

Our second attempt to get teachers to describe the operation of effective discipline avoided the apparently contentious description of colleagues. This time we asked teachers to write anonymously about an experience of their own, a lesson or part of a lesson they felt had been particularly successful. This measure was administered in two schools. Completed measures were returned by 16 per cent of the staff and 19 per cent of the staff in the different schools. This was an unsatisfactory return rate and, indeed, many of the respondents replied in generalities about preparation or personality rather than in terms of actions.

Parents were the second group we approached. Again, we did not construct a checklist of traits, but asked parents to identify their criteria in relation to their children's teachers. In addition, we wanted to know how parents had arrived at their judgements, how they gained their knowledge of the teacher they selected. We were advised against contacting parents in one of our first pair of schools; a small return was forecast. We accepted this advice, and administered our measure by post to the parents of our pupil sample in the second school. Some 200 copies of the measure were sent out with a covering letter noting the headteacher's consent and the anonymity of reply. We received eighteen replies. This was sufficiently discouraging to keep us from further attempts at eliciting parents' views, given the range of other tasks in the research. Clearly, home visits and face-to-face interviewing would have been more productive. The project's resources did not enable such visits to be undertaken.

Conclusion

We have attempted to describe the measures used in the research, the samples selected and the methods of data analysis used. We have also described measures which occupied the researchers' thought and time, but which were unproductive. Perhaps we should stress the value of piloting in relation to our successful paper-and-pencil measures; this was time-consuming but very effective in clearing the ground. The piloting of appropriate ways to carry out case-study research was highly valuable (Johnstone and Munn, 1987).

We hope that this appendix answers the questions which occur to fellow researchers reading the main text. These readers will recognise that this appendix could have been twice as long, if justice were done to the consultations, discussions, refinements and decisions made during the three years of the research.

Examples of interview schedules and the instruments used to collect data from pupils are available directly from SCRE on request.

References

Brown, S. and McIntyre, D. (1989) *Making Sense of Teaching*, Scottish Council for Research in Education, Edinburgh.

Docking, J.W. (1987) *Control and Discipline in Schools: Perspectives and Approaches*, Paul Chapman, London.

Johnstone, M. and Munn, P. (1987) *Discipline: A Pilot Study* (SCRE Project Report), Scottish Council for Research in Education, Edinburgh.

Walker, R. and Adelman, C. (1987) *A Guide to Classroom Observation*, Metheun, London.

SUBJECT INDEX